# Calling God
# "Father"

# CALLING GOD "FATHER"

## Essays on the Bible, Fatherhood and Culture

John W. Miller

*Paulist Press*
*New York/Mahwah N.J.*

Acknowledgments: Paulist Press acknowledges use of the following: "In Defense of Monotheistic Father Religion," *Journal of Religion and Health* 21/1 (Spring 1982), pp. 62–67; "The Contemporary Fathering Crisis: The Bible and Research Psychology," *The Conrad Grebel Review* (Fall 1983), pp. 21–37, used by permission of Conrad Grebel College, Waterloo, Ontario; "God as Father in the Bible and the Father Image in Several Contemporary Ancient Near East Myths: A Comparison," *Studies in Religion* 14/3 (Summer 1985), pp. 347–354, used with permission of Canadian Corporation for Studies in Religion; "Depatriarchalizing God in Biblical Interpretation: A Critique," *The Catholic Biblical Quarterly* 48/4 (October 1986), used with permission. Biblical citations are from the New Jerusalem Bible unless otherwise indicated.

*Cover design by Morris Berman Studio*

Library of Congress Cataloging-in-Publication Data

Miller, John W., 1926–
    Calling God "Father" : essays on the Bible, fatherhood, and culture / John W. Miller. — [2nd ed.]
        p.   cm.
    Includes bibliographical references and index.
    ISBN 0-8091-3897-2 (alk. paper)
    1. God—Fatherhood—Biblical teaching. 2. Fatherhood (Christian theology) 3. Bible. O.T.—Theology. I. Title.
BT153.F3M55    1999
231'.1—dc21                                                            99-36566
                                                                              CIP

Published by Paulist Press
997 Macarthur Boulevard
Mahwah, New Jersey 07430

www.paulistpress.com

Printed and bound in the
United States of America

# CONTENTS

Foreword: The Person of the Father, *David Blankenhorn*  ix

Preface to the First Edition  xv

Preface to the Second Edition  xvii

1. Introduction: Problem and Overview  3

## PART I: THEORETICAL CONSIDERATIONS

2. Origins of the Father-Involved Family  11

3. Male-Centered Reproductive Biology and
   the Dynamics of Biblical Patriarchy  18

## PART II: GOD AS FATHER IN BIBLICAL TRADITION

4. God as Father in the Bible and the Father Image
   in Several Contemporary Ancient Near Eastern Myths:
   A Comparison  35

5. Depatriarchalizing God in Biblical Interpretation:
   A Critique  45

# PART III: HUMAN FATHERING
# IN BIBLICAL TRADITION

6.  New Modes of Human Fathering (Hebrew Scriptures)      55

7.  New Modes of Human Fathering
    (New Testament Scriptures)                            71

# PART IV: CONTEMPORARY ISSUES

8.  The Contemporary Fathering Crisis:
    The Bible and Research Psychology                     87

9.  In Defense of Monotheistic Father Religion            104

10. The Refutation of the "Father" in God in Feminist
    Theologies at the End of the Twentieth Century:
    Analysis and Critique                                 110

# CONCLUSION

11. Which Way Ahead? (A Few Modest Proposals)             127


    Appendices:

    A Biblical Charter of Children's Rights: Genesis 22   137

    Epilogue: Fatherhood and Men's Studies,
    *Eugene R. August*                                    143

    Notes                                                 153

    Index                                                 191

*For Larry and Karen,*
*Emily, Jessica, and Stephanie*

*Modern society counts too easily on the domestication of man. The great upheavals of history show us that no part of his cultural adaptation is so secure that it can be relied on as a permanent human possession.\**

*Alexander Mitscherlich, *Society without the Father* (New York: Harcourt, Brace and World, 1963), p. 303.

# FOREWORD

by David Blankenhorn,

author of *Fatherless America,*
*Confronting Our Most Urgent Social Problem*

## The Person of the Father

In a forthright voice, with an obviously good heart, and with rare wisdom, John Miller has written and now reissued a small masterpiece on the relationship between human and divine fatherhood. Several years ago, I wrote a book about the crisis of fatherlessness. Professor Miller's book is much better than mine in the sense that his is far more radical; *Calling God "Father"* gets to the root of the matter.

I tried to use social science research evidence and cultural analysis to show that children need fathers and that any society such as the United States—and we could also add Canada—in which a large and growing number of adult males cease to nurture their offspring is a failing society. Professor Miller makes the same point, but goes much further. He combines practical theological insights with findings from the social sciences, particularly from the fields of anthropology and human evolutionary psychology, to reveal the foundational relationship between human fatherhood and the fatherhood of God. I only asked: Do children need fathers? Professor Miller challenges us with a much more provocative question: Do fathers need God? Or, more precisely, why and how might knowledge and love of God help a man to be a good father to his children and a good husband to his wife? Nor does Professor Miller flinch from confronting the related question

which, in our highly gender-conscious era, may be the most explosive
of all: Is it good and true that we should call God "Father"? If not, why
not? If so, why?

The more I learn about our contemporary crisis of fatherlessness,
the more I am persuaded that these are not only the hardest questions,
they are also the most important. Comparing an inquiry such as mine,
which focuses only on the social dimensions of human fatherhood, to
Professor Miller's, which directly confronts the moral and religious
essence, is like comparing near-beer to real ale, or foliage to roots. I am
certainly in Professor Miller's debt; all of us in what is now being
called the "fatherhood movement" in Canada and the United States are
in his debt.

Guided by Professor Miller's insights, and also reflecting on the
possibilities in the years ahead for reinvigorating fatherhood in North
America, let me propose three central reasons why a civilization that
expects men to nurture their offspring should also be a civilization that
recognizes the fatherhood of God. Significantly, none of these three
reasons draws our attention to male prowess, male headship, or the
strength of fatherhood. On the contrary, each underscores those
endemic male weaknesses repeatedly highlighted by Professor Miller,
especially the tendency among men toward parental waywardness and
the fragility of the father-child bond as compared to the mother-child
bond.

The first and most obvious connection between human and divine
fatherhood in North America is that the God of the Jews and Christians
has always been understood, as the Bible puts it in Psalm 10, as "the
helper of the fatherless." Across time and cultures, men abandon their
children much more frequently than do mothers. And so the urgent
question arises: What should we do—what can we do—for these children whose fathers have left them?

In the United States today, about forty percent of all children do not
live with their fathers. Before they reach age eighteen, more than half
of all U.S. children are likely to spend at least a significant portion of
their childhood living apart from their fathers. For Canada, the numbers are approximately twenty-five percent and thirty-five percent
respectively. These children are suffering. As the clinical psychologist

Judith Wallerstein so simply and powerfully puts it, they cry for their fathers. According to the social scientists, regarding nearly every problem that can be measured, these children are at significantly greater risk than are children who live with both of their parents. How can we help these suffering children? In speaking to hundreds of groups in recent years on the topic of fatherlessness, this question is probably the one that I have been asked more than any other. I have never had a satisfactory answer.

We can certainly give the mothers of these children more material resources and social support. We can also reach out directly to the children themselves, sometimes on an informal basis, and sometimes through organized mentoring and "role modeling" programs such as Big Brothers or Boys and Girls Clubs. These are good things to do. But these good works, of course, can never actually repair what is broken. They can never give these children what they are crying for: their fathers.

So I am increasingly mindful, in these situations, of the God who is Father to the fatherless. For children whose earthly fathers are all too frail and broken, there can still be the knowledge of a personal Father whose love is constant and unfailing, a Father who is "merciful and gracious, slow to anger, great in goodness and faithfulness." A Father to look up to. A pastor I know frequently begins the Sunday worship service with these words: "Don't be afraid. You are God's child in your Father's world." Children in Sunday School sing the words: "This is my Father's world, I rest me in the thought."

For many, of course, these words provide little comfort. But for the children of the covenant, even and perhaps especially the fatherless children of the covenant, knowing the fatherhood of God is an ultimate source of fatherhood. Some would argue that this assertion is pious and unrealistic, merely offering up yet another false hope for suffering children. But I wonder, which hope is more realistic? Is it realistic to hope that, say, more child support payments or more social workers will give these children what they are crying for? Better jobs for their mothers? More men who volunteer for a while as a coach or a "mentor"? For me, the answer is no. The more I think about what is truly broken and what, if anything, can truly repair it, the more I am persuaded to look to our communities of faith for the best and most realistic solutions, precisely because these communities, under God, can do what no other proposed strategy can do: they can extend to fatherless children the covenant of fatherhood.

The second connection between human fatherhood and the fatherhood of God concerns the teleology of fatherhood, or, more broadly, the teleology of adulthood. In order for a boy to grow up into a good man and become a good father, it is necessary for the boy and his society to possess a clear sense of what the end product ought to look like. Both the boy and the society require an understanding that the maturing of the male is naturally directed toward a particular end and shaped by a particular set of purposes. Otherwise, there is no way to know what it means to be a good father, or even whether becoming a father at all is a good or bad thing. Surely much of the loss of fatherhood in North America—and much of the deterioration of the adult character structure in our societies—stems precisely from what Barbara Dafoe Whitehead calls "cultural forgetting" regarding what we ultimately hope and expect men to become.

Imagine a photographer in a dark room, placing her negative in developing fluid, watching for the development of a distinct photographic image of, say, an elephant crossing a road. What is she looking for? Because she knows what an elephant crossing a road actually looks like, and because she also knows what happens when film from her camera is immersed in developing fluid, she can ultimately know with some certainty whether the particular photographic image that emerges is good or bad, either an authentic and beautiful representation of reality or not.

But what would happen if she did not know whether she had ever actually seen an elephant crossing a road? What if she were unsure of what an elephant is, or unclear as to why roads exist? What if she had only dim or contradictory ideas as to the effects of developing fluid on film? Certainly, under such circumstances, she would be virtually clueless as to whether her photograph was good or bad, or even whether she had in fact succeeded in taking a picture of an elephant crossing a road.

Similarly, we can know a good father when we see one only if we view that father essentially as an attempted representation, similar to a photograph, of a knowable external reality called fatherhood. For people of faith, the ultimate reality of "Father," in whose likeness humans are created and toward which they are ordinated, is the reality of God, the pattern of all parenthood. Absent knowledge of that reality, we inevitably become short-sighted, losing our ability to discern any larger referent that could tell us, among other things, what fathers are and what good fathers look like. We even begin to suppose that the human "photograph" by itself constitutes the whole of reality; we imagine, for example, that the human father exists on his own, apart from any transcendent order, self-owning and auto-teleological.

As John Miller shows, this form of blindness is particularly debilitating for men. Because fatherhood, much more than motherhood, is largely a matter of cultural devising, men who do not recognize the ultimate source of their fatherhood—men who, in short, do not know their Father—are especially vulnerable to the destructive and rather hard-wired male tendencies toward paternal abandonment and sexual irresponsibility. This fact, as much as any other, may help explain why we are taught to call God "Father." It is not because fathers are more important for children than mothers, and it is certainly not because men are superior to women, and thus more deserving of being divinized as a by-product of our language for God. It is rather because, across human societies, fatherhood is far weaker and more fragile than motherhood. I do not believe—and I know Professor Miller does not believe—that men need God more than women do. But I do suspect that fathers need more reminding from God than mothers do. Perhaps calling God "Father" is, in part, just such a reminder.

A third link between human and divine fatherhood concerns the realistic possibility of male submission. A central challenge facing any society—according to some anthropologists, **the** central challenge facing all human societies—is the socialization of the male: the bending of male aggression away from violence and toward pro-social purposes, especially generativity. In Judaism and Christianity, especially, part of this socialization occurs when men are taught to understand male strength as synonymous with male servanthood and self-sacrifice. (As Jesus taught in Mark 10:43–44: "...whoever would be great among you must be your servant, and whoever would be first among you must be slave of all.") But much of the socialization of the male also depends purely upon submission: the voluntary obedience of the male to a greater power, a higher authority.

And what is the final and proper source of this male submission? Surely not other men. If it were other men, the question would become merely one of my strength versus your strength, the struggle of each man against all others, the outcome of which is not civilization, but barbarism, or what political philosophers call the state of nature. Surely not women. Women are important and usually good influences on men, but women typically cannot, in this sense, compel men to obedience. There are exceptions, of course, but here is the rule: only God can cause males to fall upon their knees in voluntary submission. Or, put differently, only God the Father can teach adult males to act as his obedient sons, and therefore good husbands to their wives and good fathers to their children.

In a larger sense, of course, the relationship of human fatherhood to the fatherhood of God extends well beyond questions of submission, or of help for the fatherless, or even of a model for mature masculinity. To me probably the most important truth is that the human male, even in his weakness and short-sightedness, can come to see in his fatherhood that signal of transcendence and that spark of the divine that is in every human person. Through what Pope John Paul II once called the radiation of fatherhood, he can begin to know God and to participate with God in, well, creation.

# PREFACE TO THE FIRST EDITION

When I first wrote the following essays, I had no intention of ever publishing them as a collection. Several were drafted as lectures. "Someday," I thought, "I will try to address this subject in a less scholarly manner." When I finally attempted to do so, I found myself wondering whether the scholarly mode was not more needed. The conviction had been growing that there were important omissions and distortions in the current analysis and critique of biblical patriarchy. The feeling was also growing that these can be rectified only by a careful consideration of certain complex theoretical and exegetical issues.

It was thoughts such as these that prompted the effort to rewrite, edit and assemble these essays in a single volume. Each essay is headed with a brief synopsis of its contents. An attempt is also made in the Introduction (Chapter 1) and Conclusion (Chapter 11) to indicate how each fits into a larger pattern and what their collective relevance might be, especially for Christians.

Four of these essays were previously published in scholarly journals.[1] I thank their editors for permission to republish them here with minor revisions. I am also grateful to the adults of the Akron Mennonite Church for their helpful feedback on the occasion of our discussion of these issues at their School of Adult Studies during the summer of 1986. Ben Meyer, Elizabeth Achtemeier, Paul Nathanson, Jack Harrison, Alex Molnar, Vernard Eller and Abraham Schmidt graciously consented to read the manuscript in its penultimate form and share their comments. Their willingness to do so was greatly appreciated, as were also the substantive editorial suggestions of Fr. Lawrence Boadt.

Our daughter Karen, her husband Larry and their three children, Emily, Jessica, and Stephanie, were house guests during the weeks when I was preparing the final draft of this manuscript. Their presence in our home was a daily reminder of the importance of parenting. This book is gratefully dedicated to them and many young families like them who in the face of innumerable pressures to do otherwise are building a loving, caring life together.

# PREFACE TO THE SECOND EDITION

The essays in this new edition are much as they were in the first edition except for some minor revisions, bibliographical updating and a new essay in Chapter 10. The new essay addresses more explicitly than before the refutation of "the 'father' in God" in contemporary feminist theologies, a development I continue to believe is at the epicenter of our culture wars, signaling as it does the end of theistic religion and human culture as we have known it.[1] My goal in republishing these essays is thus the same as when they were first published a decade ago, namely, to call attention to "important omissions and distortions in the current analysis and critique of biblical patriarchy."

In the intervening years, awareness of the devastating consequences of the trends toward fatherlessness in western culture has been growing.[2] While many are hopeful these trends can be reversed, and are working creatively to that end, difficult challenges are posed by the fragility and gradual deinstitutionalization of the father-involved family in the wake of a now seemingly entrenched permissive sexual ethic.[3] In this light, clarity about the conditions necessary for the origins and emergence of the father-involved family and high cultures of fathering is more urgent than ever (see chapters 2, 3, 8, 10, 11), but recent studies of "families" in biblical culture pay little or no attention to these fundamental background issues.[4]

A criticism brought against the prior edition of this book is its seemingly disproportionate focus on fathers and sons compared to what is said about fathers and daughters. The attentive reader will discern this is not because women's needs and concerns are regarded as of lesser importance. In one way or another each of the following essays seeks to show how the emotional, social and spiritual well being of men and women are interrelated and heavily dependent on males occupying the husband-father-role in a loving, competent manner.

When encouraged by Paulist Press to consider the preparation of a new edition of these essays, I sought the advice of two people in particular whose opinions I decided would determine my response. The first was Professor Eugene August, at that time Alumni Chair in Humanities at the University of Dayton, and author of a richly annotated bibliography of *New Men's Studies* (now in its second edition). The other was David Blankenhorn, Founder and Director of the Institute of American Values (New York City) and author of an insightful, widely discussed critique of trends toward fatherlessness in North American culture. Both not only were encouraging of the proposed new edition, but also responded affirmatively to an invitation to contribute essays that might indicate its possible relevance for their respective fields of concern and expertise. This volume is enriched by their thoughtful contributions (see Prologue and Epilogue). This second edition has also benefited from the many helpful suggestions of Fr. Lawrence Boadt, Donna Crilly and their associates, as well as my wife, Louise.

# INTRODUCTION

---

*Have we not all one father?*
*Has not one God created us?*
—Malachi 2:10 (RSV).

# 1.

# Introduction:
# PROBLEM AND OVERVIEW

*Too little attention has been paid in recent critiques of biblical patriarchy to the fact that the father-involved family is a fragile cultural achievement that cannot be taken for granted. When this and other still-neglected matters are taken into consideration the precise nature of the contribution of biblical faith to a high culture of fathering can be better appreciated.*

Previously taken for granted or even eulogized, the Bible's focus on fathers is now regarded by many as patriarchal and sexist. As a consequence it has come under repeated critique and attack. Indeed, some have concluded that the Bible is so hopelessly prejudiced in this regard that there is no alternative but to abandon it. Others, still believing that biblical faith might be salvaged, have set themselves the task of changing it.

Some of the more radical changes being advocated today have to do with the biblical representation of God as father. If God is thought of as father, some argue, then males are permitted to regard themselves as godlike in ways females cannot. This is demeaning to women, they say. Thus, if we are ever to move beyond the Bible's sexist outlook, we must degenderize this notion of God either by extinguishing it, or by replacing it with gender-neutral terms such as creator, redeemer, spirit, or by balancing it with feminine images. God is to be thought of as "she" as well as "he," as "her" as well as "him."

There are still many, however, who experience innovations such as these as unsettling. How is it possible, they ask, that biblical faith, so life-giving for so many for so long, is now suddenly to be regarded as so fundamentally flawed that a virtual rewrite of its God-language is required? Were previous generations really this mistaken? Is the biblical preoccupation with fathers and fathering really as prejudicial against women as is now often assumed?

In the essays that follow I seek to address these questions by examining a number of issues that I regard as highly relevant but much neglected or overlooked in the discussions to date. The following is a brief synopsis of the topics I will be addressing.

• Many critics of biblical patriarchalism seem to assume that fatherhood in the psychological sense is something that can be taken for granted. The problem as they see it is in the excess of paternal power and prerogative that so often manifests itself. This analysis, however, is almost invariably carried out without the benefit of any conception of what in fact is involved in the male of the species taking on a paternal role in a two-parent family. Because of this it is also often not recognized that fathering is a predominantly cultural achievement, due to the fact that it is so much less nature-determined than is mothering. This is why an inevitable drift occurs in a given society in the direction of fatherless families headed by mothers alone when it fails to support the father-involved family—a situation only too familiar to those of us living in North America today. *Laying bare the pre-conditions for the emergence and continuance of a pattern of involvement of males in the care and nurture of their own children (Chapter 2) is the essential starting point for an analysis and appreciation of the contributions of biblical faith to this realm of human existence.*

• Equally neglected in recent discussion is some consideration of the dynamics of *the particular form* of the father-involved family that prevailed in the ancient Near East of biblical times. It has long been recognized that certain reproductive notions were important factors in this regard—the discovery of the role that semen plays in human reproduction, in particular. But without a prior understanding of the conditions necessary for father-involvement in the first place, as outlined in Chapter 2, the impact of this biological discovery on the formation of the two-parent family could not be properly assessed. Nor has it been sufficiently recognized how already at the dawn of the biblical period some of the more problematic features of ancient Near Eastern patriarchalism had already been identified and confronted, including the issue of a child's right to life, the *sine qua non* of a culture of fathering. These are issues I address in Chapter 3.

• In Chapters 4 and 5 the focus shifts to an analysis of the revelation of God as father in biblical tradition. Superficial assumptions regarding what this entailed and how this achievement relates to the Bible's cultural background are widespread. Many seem to think, for example, that the biblical representation of God's fatherliness simply mirrors the prevailing paternal stereotypes of the ancient Near East in which it arose. How wrong this is becomes evident, however, as one compares the biblical representation of God as father with contemporary portraits of father-gods in the myths of that region. In so doing one quickly discovers that ancient Egyptian, Canaanite or Mesopotamian religions were by no means as patriarchal as commonly assumed. *More active and powerful by far than the father-deities in these regions were son, mother and daughter deities.* Seen in this light the uniqueness of the biblical revelation becomes more tangible. A look at the biblical representation of God as father within its cultural context in antiquity is the subject of Chapter 4.

• Another misunderstanding is the now widespread belief that the Bible is not nearly as patriarchal in its representation of God as once thought. There are within the Bible itself, it is claimed, "depatriarchalizing" tendencies—texts which depict God as feminine as well as masculine, or as a deity beyond gender altogether. The evidence put forward in support of these suggestions is far from cogent, however. *Not once in biblical tradition is God ever spoken of as "she" or "her" or regarded as genderless. On the other hand, God is not portrayed there simply as male either, but as a father whose tenderness and compassion are often mother-like. In no instance does this imply that God has become a mother-figure to his worshipers. The uniformity of the canonical representation of God as father is one of its most notable features. These are the issues I address in Chapter 5.*

• Israel's faith in God as a dynamically caring father created an environment that gave birth to new modes of human fathering. This is the topic of Chapters 6 and 7. In them I seek to show how in Israel, to an extent unparalleled in the world of antiquity, faith and fatherhood came to be linked through a complex pattern of fathering rituals (such as the redemption of the firstborn, circumcision and Passover)—rituals carried out by fathers within the setting of their biological families. It was by this means, I suggest, that Israelite fathers came to be vested with an identity and a sense of care for their children that was religiously based and exceptional, giving birth in time to one of the most father-involved patterns of fatherhood on earth. This family environment was the setting within which Christianity was born, and out of which it generated its own peculiar stance toward fathering—one continuous with, and yet also different in some respects from, its Jewish heritage.

• In Chapters 8, 9 and 10, I seek to indicate some of the roots and reasons for our contemporary fatherhood crisis and how the biblical tradition of fathering may be relevant to our efforts at surmounting it. It is at this point that my essays become most explicitly apologetic. Not only, I argue, is there a remarkable congruence between the Bible and modern research psychology in their mutual attitudes toward fathering and its importance, but viewed in the light of what we now know about the psychological development of children of both sexes, one can begin to sense why the biblical revelation of God's gracious fatherliness has in fact been such a blessing for the communities worldwide that have embraced it. As biblical law codes and covenants so confidently declare, those shall live long in the land who follow this God and his precepts. The dangerous consequences of certain fault-lines in feminist theologies that seek to refute the "father" in God become evident in this light and are discussed in my new essay on this subject in Chapter 10.

• My final essay (Chapter 11) is an attempt at indicating the possible relevance of the prior essays by asking what in this light some of the more obvious weaknesses and strengths of North American Christians might be, so far as a recovery of stronger fatherhood traditions is concerned. The way ahead will not be easy, I suggest, due in part to certain inherently ambivalent attitudes toward the father-involved family in western democratic traditions, as well as within Christianity itself. The western democratic ideals of equality and freedom are not necessarily congenial to family values, and Christianity has traditionally paid more attention to the needs of the spiritual family of the church than to developing a spiritual support system for the biological family. Nevertheless, there are specific things we might be doing, and my study concludes with a few suggestions of what some of these might be.

# PART ONE
# THEORETICAL CONSIDERATIONS

---

*Simply stated, an adult female will be naturally trans-
formed into a social mother when she bears a child,
but there is no corresponding natural transformation
for a male.\**

\*Peter Wilson, *Man the Promising Primate: The Conditions of Human
Evolution*, Second Edition (New Haven: Yale University Press, 1983), p. 71.

# 2.

# ORIGINS OF THE FATHER-INVOLVED FAMILY

*Due to the marginality of males in the reproductive process, fathering is a cultural acquisition to an extent that mothering is not. Hence, when a culture ceases to support a father's involvement with his own children (through its laws, mores, symbols, models, rituals) powerful natural forces take over in favor of the mother-alone family.*

Powerful trends in our culture are calling into question prior traditions regarding fathers.[1] In attacking "patriarchy" and calling for equality of the sexes some feminists appear to want to discredit the significance of gender distinctions altogether.[2] At the same time there is growing alarm over births to out-of-wedlock teenagers, marriage breakdown and the multiplication of single-parent, mother-led families. We are approaching the point, statisticians tell us, when almost half of all North American children will be raised in such essentially fatherless families for some part of their lives.[3] In reaction, we are witnessing a fresh wave of interest among social scientists and scholars in fathering and the father's role in the emotional development of children.[4] Caught between these conflicting trends, many are in a state of confusion. Are fathers important or not? If important, in what sense, and why is it seemingly so difficult for fathers to assume their proper roles in their families as caretakers of children?[5]

One major source of our confusion would appear to be the inadequate picture we have of the origins of the "father-involved" family.

Contrary to prevailing assumptions "fatherhood" is not something that can be taken for granted. Neither in the world of antiquity nor today are males necessarily the involved, "in charge" figures patriarchal theory portrays them as being—certainly not if by this is meant any signifi- cant role as patriarchs or fathers in the care and training of their own children.[6] In the myths of the ancient world, for example, it is not the father-deities who are thought of as ruling the world, but their wives, sons and daughters.[7] That therefore God should be thought of in bibli- cal faith as involved, gracious, "redemptive" father (Is 63:16) is also not to be taken for granted.[8]

How then did the father-involved family originate?

## Theoretical Considerations

Due to the fragmentary nature of the historical data bearing on this issue, it may be well to begin our discussion of this question with cer- tain theoretical considerations first of all. As a number of researchers have already recognized, an adequate hypothesis in this regard must begin with a recognition of the degree to which fathering is a largely cultural acquisition due to the marginality of males in the reproductive process.[9] After sexual intercourse there is no *biologically* compelling reason for the male to have anything further to do with the child he may have engendered. Rather, from the moment of conception onward the growth of the fetus is solely the affair of the female. For nine months it develops in her womb and then is born of her body and suckles at her breasts. A female may choose to abort her child, or abandon it at birth, but if she allows biology to take its course, she will become a mother to her child by an inevitable natural process. Nature does not dictate to the same degree what a male's role shall be in the life of his child.

Looked at from this perspective, it is apparent that for there to be fatherhood in a *more than* biological sense, a set of overlapping, largely cultural developments were (and are) required.

First, a scientific discovery had to be made. Human beings had to become conscious of the link that exists between a specific act of sexual intercourse and the gestation and birth of a child nine months later.[10]

Only when that link had been established could the children born to a certain mother be recognized as belonging to a specific father as well. This recognition must have been slow in coming, since not every sexual act leads to a pregnancy. Indeed, there are primitive tribes even today (or there were just a few years ago), such as the Melanesian Trobrianders described by Malinowski, where this truth has not yet dawned.[11] Among them a woman is thought of as bearing children of herself (once her womb has been opened) through the implantation and reincarnation of departed spirits. This being so, her male companion is not regarded as the father of her children, but as "husband of my mother" (as the children refer to him), or even as "stranger" or "outsider." As a consequence, "between the father and the children there is no union whatsoever," Malinowski writes.[12] Children are regarded instead as belonging exclusively to the mother and her extended family, and come into the custody of the mother's brother as they grow older. From this we can see how critical was the discovery of male involvement in reproduction for the formation of father-involved families. Apart from this discovery and its cultural appropriation, fatherhood in the sense of a male's involvement with his own children as father does not exist at all.

However, even with such an awareness firmly in place, as we know it was, for example, in the ancient Near East, and in Greece, already in the second millennium B.C.E.,[13] an additional development had to occur for the father-involved family to become an established institution. If a given child is to be recognized as the offspring of a specific male (and not just of the female), bonds are needed between individual men and women that are sexually exclusive. Only in that way is a given male able to know that the children born to a certain woman are truly his and not someone else's. Furthermore, this pair-bonding of male and female must be sufficiently durable to insure that the male involved will be present nine months later when his child is born, not to speak of his availability during the years when his children are growing to maturity. In other words, *psychological* fathering by a child's own father is only possible within a carefully regulated framework of sexual relations between specific men and women extending over the period of time the children are being born and growing to maturity.[14]

But even with this, a given male's actual care of his own children is by no means assured. In addition to knowing *how* children are generated, and in addition to *being there* as they are born and growing up, an equally momentous transformation was required in the *mutual attitudes* of the males and females involved toward these offspring. Now that *two* parents are present instead of one, the females, who until this time had regarded the children born to them as *theirs* exclusively (by virtue of their only too obvious role in their gestation and birth), must now begin to defer to the males, granting them too a share in the ownership of these children. And the males on their part, in spite of being outsiders to the whole birthing process, must also begin now to accept this new role—taking ownership and responsibility and sharing in their children's care.[15]

"Simply stated," writes Wilson, upon whose analysis of these issues I have relied for the prior description,[16]

> an adult female will be naturally transformed into a social mother when she bears a child, but there is no corresponding natural transformation for a male. If he becomes a social father he does so only culturally or symbolically and, as it were, by permission of the female....Only if we bear in mind this meaning of "father" [he adds] and the vulnerability of the father to nature and the female can we explain the dominance of the male/father in all human cultures, which can first be seen in the asymmetry between the relations of mother/offspring and father/offspring.

To summarize: in that a child grows in the body of its mother, mothering is a biologically determined experience to a far greater extent than is fathering. By contrast, fathering is a predominantly cultural acquisition. Its prerequisites are the discovery of the male role in reproduction, the cultural appropriation of that discovery, the formation of exclusive, enduring sexual bonds between a specific male and female, and their mutual willingness to share in the ownership and care of the children born to them. Seen in this light the historical emergence of the father-involved family may be characterized as a truly revolutionary event.

## Historical Considerations

When and how did this revolution occur? As to when, a look around us at our own culture should convince us that it would be wrong to say it has even yet occurred. It is still occurring. We are in the midst of it. The ease with which we have recently adopted the "new morality" of the sexual revolution and are now prepared, apparently, to live with its consequences (high abortion rates, epidemic venereal disease, high divorce rates, an enormous increase in mother-led families where fathers are present hardly at all) should be evidence enough that the father-involved family is indeed a recent, still imperfectly realized cultural and spiritual acquisition.

A glance at our primitive past and the world of the higher primates confirms this analysis. While the industrial and sexual revolutions have intensified the problems with fathering in modern societies,[17] a careful study of most human cultures will reveal profound difficulties in this area.[18] And when we look even further back into prehistoric cultures and the world of the higher primates, this is even more the case. In many primitive societies, for example, men typically have several wives living in separate houses who are almost totally responsible for the care of the children born to them. Only after traumatic puberty rituals are these children wrenched loose from their maternal environment and integrated into the world of the fathers.[19] Still further back in our pre-hominid past among the higher primates, fathering is even less in evidence, it seems, and among the lower orders of life almost non-existent.[20]

When and how then *did* fathering begin? The Bible itself suggests an answer that is remarkably congruent with the findings of modern ethnologists. In Genesis 2:4b–25 the deceptively childlike story is told of the creation of the first man and women. In it we are informed that while the male of our species, Adam, was created first, he was not happy or complete. Consequently a search was begun to find him a companion. It was then that the animals were created, but none was able to assuage his loneliness. This was the moment, the story declares, when Yahweh-elohim put Adam to sleep and from his side took a rib and created woman—and when the man awoke and saw what God had done, he exclaimed, "This one at last is bone of my bones and flesh of my flesh!" The story concludes with this climactic line: "This is why a man leaves his father and mother and becomes attached to his wife, and they become one flesh" (Gn 2:24).

This text which was quoted approvingly by Jesus (Mk 10:7–9), and in this way has become the marital ideal of Christianity together with Judaism, is a perfectly frank and lucid acknowledgment of the heightened role that heterosexuality plays among humans as compared to animals.[21] Among the higher primates heterosexual relating occurs, for the most part, randomly and sporadically—only at the specific and often limited time of the female estrus. As a result sexual intercourse is an impersonal, episodic, socially and psychologically marginal and inconsequential event. A decisive step in the direction of psychological fathering occurred when "woman" was created—that is, with the phasing out of the restricted estrus in women and the emergence of an enlarged capacity for personal sexual bonding on the part of both men and women. Anthropologist Helen Fisher, on the basis of the discovery of skeletal remains of a family group along the Hadar River of the Afar Triangle of Ethiopia, believes such bonding may have occurred (and males were thus incorporated into the female group) as early as four million years ago.[22] "Yet," she adds, "these males, lacking an awareness of paternity, had an ancient tendency to desert their mates. So youngsters still associated their heritage with mother. But by now the seeds of kinship had been planted.[23]

This insight of both the Bible and modern ethnology not only highlights the necessity (previously noted) of this type of bond arising for fathering to occur, but indicates that a uniquely *human* sexuality had first to emerge for this to happen. Without more enduring personal-sexual bonds between individual men and women there could be no fathering. Without a heightened capacity for sexual relating there would likely not have arisen that unique human capacity for forging such bonds.

## Concluding Comments

With this in mind one might say that fathering too is of nature to some degree at least—that is, with the rise of a uniquely human capacity for sexual bonding, there was also now a natural incentive for men and women to remain together to care for the children their sexual relations had engendered. However, this pair-bond of mother and father was (and is) notoriously fragile in comparison with the bond between mother and child. In this sense, mothering is far more profoundly nature-determined than is fathering. *Hence, where a culture ceases to support, through its mores, symbols, models, laws and rituals, the sanctity of the sexual bond between a man and his wife and a father's involvement with his own children, powerful natural forces will inevitably take over in favor of the mother-alone family; the fragility of the sexual bond (and the investment of fathers with children) will give way to the strength of the primary bond between mother and child.*

It is in this sense that the father-involved family must be viewed as a cultural artifact, a creation of the human species—some would argue, the definitive cultural artifact that lies at the foundation of all other cultural achievements and most uniquely distinguishes what it means to be human from other forms of life on this planet.[24] Intuitively, in Genesis 2, in its characterization of the advent of woman as partner to man as the crowning act of the creation story, the Bible alludes to this historic development. Only when this had happened could human history as such begin.

# 3.

# MALE-CENTERED REPRODUCTIVE BIOLOGY AND THE DYNAMICS OF BIBLICAL PATRIARCHY

*The discovery (as it was thought) that life originates in male semen had a revolutionary impact on the form of the family in the cultures of the ancient Near East. It not only solidified the role of fathers in families, but increased the potential for wife and child abuse. However, steps were taken early on to curtail such abuse both outside and within biblical culture.*

The family histories in Genesis which trace the origins of peoples, including the biblical people, reflect a quite specific stage in the emergence of the father-involved family in the ancient Near East during the third and second millennia B.C.E. The families of this period and region are now generally regarded as "patriarchal," which literally translated refers to the father *(pater)* as "beginning" or "first" *(arche)* and to the tracing of lineage through the male line. Once a title of honor (Acts 2:27) "patriarch" has more recently come to be viewed in a negative light as signifying an excess or abuse of male prerogative and power.[1]

What I wish to indicate in this essay, however, is that the patriarchy of this era, when viewed from the perspective of the conditions essential to a male's involvement in family life, may be judged to have had both a negative *and* a positive side to it, and that especially in that cycle of stories, beginning with Genesis 12, that informs us of the origins of the biblical people, testimony is given to a momentous break with certain darker aspects of the patriarchal heritage of that region and period at one very crucial point: in the story of Abraham's near-sacrifice of his son Isaac (Gn 22:1–18) the legitimacy of a father's right to kill his own child is directly spoken to and challenged for the first time in history, so far as we know.

In order to appreciate what was involved in this breakthrough, and how important it was, it will be necessary first of all, however, to take a careful look at the cultural framework which allowed fathers to have such absolute power over their children in the first place. A primary factor in this development appears to have been the discovery of the male role in a child's conception. An analysis of this matter will not only afford us insights into the dynamics of ancient Near Eastern patriarchy, but assist us in appreciating what it meant for the biblical people to challenge, moderate and utilize this cultural setting for the advances in father-involvement that would follow.

## Reproductive Theory

The conception of a child was a mysterious event for the peoples of antiquity. "I do not know how you appeared in my womb," testifies the mother of the seven Maccabean martyrs (2 Mc 7:22). "You do not understand how the wind blows, or how the embryo grows in a woman's womb," writes the venerable Qoheleth, "no more can you understand the work of God, the Creator of all" (Eccl 11:5). An aspect of this mystery was the sexual act itself. Its connection with pregnancy and the birth of a child nine months later was by no means apparent. Indeed, it is not improbable that the earliest thinking regarding pregnancy and birth bypassed the male involvement altogether and regarded women as generating children *by themselves* with the help of God. This appears to be the context within which the veneration of the mother-goddess in the Neolithic and Chalcolithic periods proliferated.[2]

The reproductive theory that replaced this one in the ancient Near East as early as the third millennium B.C.E. is most clearly spelled out in the works of the fourth-century Athenian philosopher, Aristotle. In a rather lengthy essay entitled "The Generation of Animals," he draws a distinction between male and female on the basis of the fluids they emit: menstrual fluid in the case of the female, semen in males. It follows, he writes, that "Male is that which is able to concoct, to cause to take shape, and to discharge semen possessing the 'principle' of the 'form'," whereas "female is that which receives semen, but is unable to cause semen to take shape or discharge it."[3]

What this suggests is an understanding of the reproductive process that is almost the opposite of the earlier point of view. Far from the mother being thought of as primary (or even sole) source of the child she bears, it is the male now who is viewed as producing that which is essential to the creation of children. The consequences of this new understanding for family law, Gerda Lerner has noted in her book *The Creation of Patriarchy*, are spelled out in "The Furies," the last play in the "Oresteia" trilogy by Aeschylus, where the playwright lets Apollo settle an argument over mother-right by declaring:[4]

> The mother is not the parent of the child
> which is called hers. She is the nurse who tends
> the growth
> Of young seed planted by its true parent,
> the male.

The likening of semen to seed in this passage is one that reappears with some frequency in biblical sources. Thus Abraham is told that "your heir will be the issue [semen] of your own body" (Gn 15:4). Subsequently, Abraham was led outside, shown the stars, and promised: "Just so will your descendants [seed] be" (15:5, 18). Thus, in exact accordance with Aristotelian reproductive biology, Isaac is here regarded as coming forth from his father's body (not his mother's).

If male sexual discharge is now regarded as "seed," it follows that the female womb is understood as "ground" of sorts into which the seed is planted. Job 10:10–11 likens semen to a substance that was poured out "like milk," then allowed to "thicken like curds" (in the womb), at which point it was then clothed with skin and flesh and woven with bone and sinew (see also Ps 139:13). A similar picture of conception is drawn in the first-century B.C.E. book of Wisdom, where King Solomon is quoted as saying:

> I was modeled in flesh inside a mother's womb,
> where, for ten [lunar] months, in blood I acquired
> substance—
> the result of virile seed and pleasure,
> sleep's companion (Wis 7:1–2).

The first-century B.C.E. Jewish philosopher Philo echoes this conception when he writes:[5]

> Now seed is the original starting-point of living creatures. That this is a substance of a very low order, resembling foam, is evident to the eye. But when it has been deposited in the womb and become solid, it acquires movement, and at once enters upon natural growth.

At this point yet in the science of reproductive biology "there is of course no thought of the part played by the ovum," David Mace observes. "The new individual is fashioned solely out of the impregnating principle provided by the father, at the behest of Yahweh....The womb of the mother simply constitutes the receptacle within which God works His mysterious miracle."[6] The persistence of such reproductive concepts in Middle Eastern culture down to modern times is indicated by a reference in the eighth-century Quran to a child being fashioned by Allah from a "sperm drop" (Sura XVIII: 37).

David Mace has noted how consistent this reproductive view is with the biblical principle of succession from father to son, for if children originate in the "seed" of the father, then "the continuity of the 'line' can logically exist only through the males of the family," and

> the particular woman who happens to bear sons to a man is from the point of view of succession a matter of indifference; hence the complete absence in Hebrew thought of our modern conceptions of "legitimacy." The woman supplies nothing of her essential self

to the new being. She merely provides in her womb the human incubator in which the man's seed becomes his child, the reproduction of his image.[7]

More might be said, but from the data already surveyed it seems evident that a quite specific set of prescientific biological concepts contributed to the emergence and shape of that unique form of father involvement that prevailed in the ancient Near East during the third and second millennia B.C.E.

## An Assessment

What needs to be evaluated, however, is what the social consequences of this were and are. Two contrasting assessments of this development have been put forward by researchers to date. The Canadian psychologist David Bakan, for example, appears to regard it as essentially a positive one in that it enabled men in particular to overcome what he terms a "crisis of paternalization"—that is, the generic reluctance among males to involve themselves in the ownership and care of their own children. "If the seed is that of the male, if it is his property," he writes, "then it is essential to develop social methods of guaranteeing female fidelity in marriage and virginity prior to marriage," in order to guarantee "that the offspring of the female are the offspring of the male." Then too the male will begin assuming "obligations of maintenance, protection, and education of the offspring, which prior to this have been associated with the female."[8]

The feminist historian Gerda Lerner evaluates this same set of events quite differently. In the wake of the discovery of the male role in reproduction, she writes, there did indeed occur a development in which men came to have exclusive rights to the sexuality of certain females, but in making themselves subservient sexually in this manner, women lost their autonomy and became subordinate to males as a group, and children too came under the autocratic authority of the father.[9] In fact, Lerner argues, here lie the origins of that excessive patriarchalism that remains to this day such a blight on the world. Thus, only as women take back ownership and control of their sexuality, she insists, will they achieve the strength, identity and autonomy needed to move beyond patriarchy and rectify its abuses.[10] Erudite and detailed as her analysis is, however, she does not tell us how this can be done without bringing to an end the involvement of men in the fathering of their own children.[11]

There is truth, it seems, in both of these assessments. If the reproductive biology outlined above did not recognize sufficiently the genetic contributions of the female to the child she bore, looked at in the light of the conditions necessary for fatherhood (knowledge of the male role in reproduction, and an enduring and exclusive bond on the part of the male with a female partner),[12] it must be judged a valuable development insofar as it strengthened the heretofore fragile relations of men to their wives and offspring, and in this way gave rise to a particularly solid and tenacious form of father-involvement in the reproduction of the species. With the procreative biology outlined above in place, any questions as to a father's rightful share in the fruit of his wife's womb were swept aside. While the child was still obviously the mother's in that her body provided the indispensable matrix for its gestation and growth, it was clearly also now the father's as well (and uniquely so), in that it originated in his body from his semen.

I concur therefore with Bakan that the general impact of this reproductive concept (flawed though it was) was a positive one. It helped males overcome a species-wide developmental crisis in paternalization, and provided a solid foundation for the emergence of fatherhood as a distinctively human attribute and institution.

Nevertheless, it must also be acknowledged (in agreement with Lerner) that this biological perspective could and did contribute to the emergence of exaggerated notions of paternal power and authority in the nuclear family, which, if unregulated, could (and did) result in abuses on the father's part against other members of his family. In what follows I will try to indicate that the potential for *wife abuse* under these circumstances was already long recognized in ancient Near Eastern culture prior to the rise of biblical culture, and that steps had been taken to protect against this. Unfortunately, the same cannot be said regarding the potential for *child abuse*. Abuse of children was all too commonplace in the ancient Near East, including their outright slaughter. It is precisely for this reason that the stories that open the biblical record, particularly the account in Genesis 22 that tells of Abraham's break with the prevailing notions of child sacrifice, are of such great significance for the future of the father-involved family.

## 1. Protection against Wife Abuse

With the advent of a biology that understood the male sexual effluent as the point of origin of a child, fidelity in sexual relations became imperative. While male-female sexual bonding had been a distinctive human trait long prior to this (see the discussion of this point in Chapter 2), the importance now attaching to the exclusivity of such bonds became suddenly and dramatically apparent. Only if a given male had sole and exclusive rights to a specific female's womb could he be certain that the children born to her would be his and not someone else's. Consequently, in all ancient Near Eastern law codes, including the biblical codes, adultery (sexual relations between a man's wife and a male other than her husband) is regarded as a crime punishable by death (see, for example, *Code of Hammurabi* 129; Lv 20:10).

This stipulation, however (that a wife's sexuality belongs exclusively to her husband), could have as one of its consequences that the husband might begin thinking of his wife as a possession to do with as he pleased. As just suggested, however, this category of problem was recognized and addressed quite early in the ancient Near East. In the eighteenth century B.C.E. *Code of Hammurabi* (CH), for example, there is a large section of laws pertaining to points of contention between the partners of a marriage with respect to their mutual and individual rights (see laws 128–195), and even a cursory reading of these texts will indicate how then already, the distinctions were drawn between marital-sexual rights, on the one hand, and the rights of husbands and wives as persons, on the other. No more was a *wife* regarded as her husband's possession to do with as he pleased than was *he* regarded as the wife's possession to do with as she pleased. *Both* parties to a marriage needed protection from abuse by the other, these laws imply, but the larger number of laws devoted to the rights of wives does suggest that women especially were vulnerable to abuse and were in need of help in this regard. However, such help was forthcoming, it seems, in the legal traditions and mores of this region.[13]

A husband, for example, was not permitted to sell his wife into slavery. Nor is there any hint of a privileged position on his part that would excuse him for physically abusing her. The worst that a man could do to a wife who displeased him (or failed to bear him a child) was to divorce her; even then, however (according to the *Code of Hammurabi*), he had to give her "the full amount of her marriage price" (the sum of money he had given her father in compensation at the time of marriage), plus the dowry she had brought with her into the marriage (CH 138). The Hammurabi Code also permits a wife to leave her husband should she come to hate him, and if upon investigation her displeasure was shown to be justified, she could even take her dowry with her (CH 142). Even a woman who humiliates and neglects her husband, due to her too many business activities outside the home, is not punished on this account, except that her husband was then permitted to marry a second wife, and her status in the home was reduced to that of a maidservant (CH 141).

It should also be kept in mind that marriages in this culture were not the affair of two people only, but of their families, clans and villages, and were in this way monitored for potential abuses and injustices by a wider community. The very ancient practice of a compensatory payment to the wife's family by the bridegroom is but one example of this wider accountability of the marital couple, as is the provision by the wife's family of a dowry for their daughter—that is, a sum of wealth which was hers to keep as her own even after she moved into her husband's house. This latter (her dowry) may be regarded as her family's attempt at providing her with at least some economic self-sufficiency, even though married.

Biblical culture and law reflect these traditions. There too a dowry was customary (Gn 31:14–16), it seems, and a man's freeborn wife was clearly not her husband's possession to do with as he pleased. He did not own her as one owns a slave (unless, of course, she was in fact a slave-wife).[14] In biblical law too the worst thing he might do, should she displease him, would be to divorce her, at which point she was free to marry someone else (see Dt 24:1–3).

This is not to deny, however, that even in this area there were ongoing problems of a subtler kind that continued to plague this relationship (and still do). While heightening the importance of virginity and fidelity (a sine qua non if men were to know who their children were), the new awareness of the male role in reproduction did not similarly clarify the issue of how many wives a man might have. Nor did it lead at once to a resolution of what attitude should be taken toward prostitution, sacred or otherwise. Also, in a culture where slavery was still widespread, there were issues to contend with regarding the incorporation of slave wives into a man's household.

Even a glance at biblical narrative and law will indicate the degree to which issues of this kind remained problematic almost to the end of the biblical period. Thus, the founder of the biblical people, Abraham, is portrayed in Genesis as taking to wife not just Sarah, but her slave girl (Gn 16), and Abraham's grandson, Jacob, inadvertently becomes the husband of two wives, not just one (Gn 29). In another ancient story, Judah, forefather of the tribe of Judah, is said to have had intercourse with someone he thought to be a prostitute, but who he later learned was his daughter-in-law (Gn 38). The practice of having slaves for wives, and a plurality of wives, is implied in Israel's oldest law code (Ex 21:7–11). Later on Israel's greatest king, David, took to himself numerous wives and concubines (2 Sam 5:13), and his son Solomon, even more (1 Kgs 11:1–3).

Only gradually, it seems, did there emerge within human culture generally, and within biblical culture specifically, the recognition that the monogamous fidelity required of a wife is the ideal for husband as well (see the admonitions and teachings in this regard in Gn 2:22–25; Prv 5; 7:6–27; Mal 2:13–16; Mk 10:1–12), and that random sexual relations apart from a marital intent (prostitution) are dehumanizing (Hos 4:14; Prv 29:3; 1 Cor 6:15f).

## 2. The Vulnerability of Children

The other relation both positively and negatively affected by the advent of male-centered reproductive biology was that of the father's relation to his children. The impact of the new biological views in *this* regard, it seems, was even greater than its impact on wife-husband relations, for men and women had been *sexually* bonding for millennia prior to the advent of a specific reproductive theory that ascribed procreativity to the male.[15] So far as that relationship was concerned, therefore, an androcentric reproductive concept simply added to the significance of this bond and further strengthened it by accenting how important was the male contribution to the reproductive process. However, the impact of this new biological understanding upon how the children themselves were now viewed must have been nothing short of revolutionary, for prior to this children were regarded as belonging exclusively to the mother (in that they were thought to have originated solely from her), whereas now they were viewed as originating solely from the father.

It was this traumatic reversal of perspective, we may conjecture, that laid the foundation for the famous *patria potestas* (power of the father) which in ancient Roman culture reached its zenith in fathers being given the right by law even to kill their children, should they wish to do so.[16] Coming as it did from his loins, the child was now thought of as belonging to the father to do with as he wished. Indeed, in Babylonian law children were so much linked to the father that sons could be punished for their father's crimes. Even in biblical law a striking difference can be noted between the authority a father had over his children in comparison to his authority over his wife. As noted, he was *not* permitted to sell his wife into slavery; she was not his property to dispose of as he wished. But he *was* permitted to sell his children (see, for example, Ex 21:7). Was he also permitted to *kill* them (as were Roman fathers of antiquity)?

These questions are crucially important ones for assessing the impact of biblical faith on the prevailing culture of fatherhood, and for sensing how at this point too it began forging a new way. However to gain a proper appreciation of the significance of these developments, it will be necessary to digress a bit and note how pervasive in antiquity was the practice of killing children, and also how deep-seated were the rationalizations for doing so.

## Infanticide and Child Sacrifice

One of the most gruesome consequences of the notion that a father owned his children (because of their having originated from his body) was the practice of infanticide and child sacrifice in the cultures of antiquity. This is a skeleton in the closet of humanity that we dare not ignore if we are to grasp the severity of the problems that even today yet must be surmounted if we are ever to be successful in civilizing the father-involved family.

Since the literature on this subject is extensive (and can be readily consulted by anyone interested in knowing more about it), I will confine myself here to a few examples only.[17] In ancient Rome, children at birth were regularly laid at their father's feet for his decision as to whether they should live or die. If he lifted them up, they would live; if left on the ground, they would be taken away and exposed to die in some predetermined place. It was from this pool of abandoned children that the slaves and prostitutes of ancient cultures were often drawn.

So widespread was infanticide in ancient Greece that historians of antiquity saw it as the chief reason for the decline of Hellenistic culture. But not only among the Greeks and Romans were such practices rife— all over the Mediterranean region in this period infanticide and child sacrifice were rampant. Of the Carthaginians Plutarch wrote (in his *De superstitione*) that they slew their children "as if they were lambs or chickens....They placed them one by one, on the sloping hands of the brazen image, from which they rolled into the pit of fire....The mothers had to stand by and see it done without a tear or groan."

The Bible itself testifies to the prevalence of such gruesome rituals. 2 Kings 3:26–27, for example, tells of a Moabite king who sacrificed his son, and Deuteronomy 12:31 indicates that practices of this kind were also common among the Canaanites. Indeed, even Israelite fathers, we are told, did such things too during the kingship period, after Solomon ceased being a wholehearted follower of the God of Israel (Yahweh) and permitted other gods to be worshiped on the mountain to the east of Jerusalem (see 1 Kgs 11:7; Jer 7:31–34; 19:5–25; 32:35–36); at least two Israelite kings are said to have sacrificed their first-born sons (2 Kgs 16:3; 21:6. See also 1 Kgs 16:34).

Why? What motivated fathers to slaughter their own children in this seemingly senseless manner? In seeking an answer, one notes, to begin with, the assumption that they had the right to do so. Nowhere in the cultures of antiquity outside of Israel was this right challenged, so far as we know. The rationalizations for such conduct were, as a result, free to proliferate and could be quite varied, it seems. *Religious* motives predominated in some instances. For example, if animal sacrifices were efficacious for the atonement of sins, it was imagined, how much more the sacrifice of one's own children, and one's first-born above all!

With what shall I enter Yahweh's presence
and bow down before God All-high?
Shall I enter with burnt offerings,
with calves one year old?
Will he be pleased with rams by the thousand,
with ten thousand streams of oil?
Shall I offer my eldest son for my wrong-doing,
the child of my own body for my sin?
(Mi 6:6–7).

In other instances children were killed simply as a means of birth control, much as today abortion is practiced. A letter written in 1 B.C.E. by an Egyptian migrant laborer named Hilarion, to his wife, Alis, pregnant with his second child, advises her, "If by chance you bear a child, if it is a boy, let it be; if it is a girl, cast it out…" (*Papyrus Oxyhynchus* 744). More complex psychological dynamics, such as paternal irritation, fear or hatred, could also be involved. In a famous creation myth from Mesopotamia the father-deity, Apsu, is characterized as so maddened by the noisiness of his offspring that he determined to kill them to keep them from disturbing his sleep! Such trivial paternal irritations might be intensified by alliances between children and their mothers against the fathers. Such is the theme of the biblical story of the collusion of Rebekah and Jacob against Isaac (Gn 27), a tale reminiscent of the Oedipus Rex legends of Greece. In these latter a son, abandoned by his father, inadvertently murders him and marries his mother. In certain primitive cultures, paternal dread of something like this happening was so great that a ritual funeral for the father was enacted during his wife's pregnancy. For similar reasons firstborn sons in certain Ugandan tribes were, until recently, choked to death by attending midwives with the father's implicit permission.

From all this it is apparent that if the advent of the father-involved family brought blessing, it also brought turmoil and tragedy. Not just one but *two* people were now intimately involved in *shared* ownership and care of the children born to them. Prior to this a child belonged to the mother alone, and her maternal instincts helped to guarantee its protection and care. But now that a father was also present—now that it was understood that the child belonged to him as well (and not just to the mother)—would *he also* protect and nurture it with a degree of love and concern that matched hers? Would he also, *as father*, be mother-like to his children, and truly care for them?

## Intimations of Another Way: Genesis 22

Just as we can trace a development within biblical culture corrective of some of the possible abuses of spouses toward one another (and in the direction of monogamy and marital fidelity on the part of women *and* men), so we can also identify developments there in the direction of greater protection of children. Such, I suggest, is the significance of that moving account that stands at the apex and conclusion of the Abraham stories in Genesis: the one in Genesis 22 that relates the gripping episode of Abraham's near-sacrifice of his only son Isaac. This particular story opens with a command from God to Abraham to sacrifice his son, a command which Abraham sets out to obey *only too willingly*, it seems. At the critical moment, however, his hand is stayed, and he is ordered not to harm his son after all, for what God wanted, we learn, was not *Isaac's* actual sacrifice, but something from *Abraham*—his inner awe and respect, and that only (Gn 22:12). Although not legislation in the strict sense of the word, the commandment from heaven at this story's climactic conclusion not to kill his son or do him any harm (Gn 22:12) is the first definitive declaration we know of delimiting the authority of a father over his children and prohibiting him from taking his child's life.[18] As such, this narrative may be regarded as a first charter of children's rights (see the essay in the Appendix for a fuller exposition of this text from this perspective). Only when this point had been clarified (that fathers must not arbitrarily kill or harm their children for any reason) could a culture of fatherhood begin to flourish, as it subsequently did in biblical tradition.[19]

# Summary

An especially tenacious form of father-involved family came to birth in the ancient Near East in the wake of the discovery of the male role in reproduction. This discovery had a twofold impact: it consolidated paternal consciousness and the rights of fathers to exclusive sexual access to specific women and to their own children (codified in a growing body of laws and customs in support of marital fidelity); at the same time, wives and children became more vulnerable to abuse of paternal authority.

Potential abuses of wives (or husbands) within the marital relationship were already identified and dealt with in the marital laws and traditions of the ancient Near East generally. In this regard biblical tradition at the beginning simply reflected its wider cultural background. On the other hand, biblical faith would early on become innovative in the face of child abuse. As the story of Abraham's near sacrifice of his only son Isaac so powerfully intimates, already the patriarchs of the Bible began to break with their culture at one very crucial point: they came to see that the sacrificial slaughter of children by their fathers was not what God wanted.

# PART TWO
# GOD AS FATHER IN
# BIBLICAL TRADITION

---

*The God of Judaism is undoubtedly a father-symbol and father-image, possibly the greatest such symbol and image conceived by man. Nor can there be any doubt as to the psychological need answered by this image. This, together with the great moral imperatives, was the unique contribution of prophetic Judaism to mankind.\**

*Raphael Patai, *The Hebrew Goddess* (New York: Avon Books, 1967), p. 9.

# 4.

# GOD AS FATHER IN THE BIBLE AND THE FATHER IMAGE IN SEVERAL CONTEMPORARY ANCIENT NEAR EASTERN MYTHS: A COMPARISON

*The assumption that biblical father religion is simply continuous with wider ancient Near Eastern patriarchalism is unsupported by a comparison of the portrait of God as father in the Bible with divine father figures in several contemporary ancient Near Eastern mythologies. Only in biblical tradition is it believed that a father-god truly worthy of being hallowed is fully in charge of the cosmic home.*

If, as has been argued, myths like dreams are "symbolic of the dynamics of the psyche,"[1] and "modal familial experiences…play an important part in shaping the fantasy products of a culture,"[2] it would appear that the peoples of the ancient Near East during the second millennium B.C.E. were experiencing a fathering crisis of sorts. In many of their myths, in any case, fathers present problems. Their marginality, cruelty, incompetence, and powerlessness, more often than not, pose dilemmas to which mother, son or daughter deities must respond either by defending themselves or by taking action to uphold the universe in their stead.[3] Only in biblical myth, it seems, is there a divine father who is a major force for good in the life of the world. This raises the question whether biblical faith in God as father, often said to reflect an already established patriarchal order, may not instead have arisen on the wings of an emotional/spiritual revolution.[4]

My purpose in this chapter is not, however, primarily to search out how or why this happened, but simply to highlight a few of the more important comparisons and contrasts that can be drawn when looking at the portrait of God as father in the Bible against the backdrop of divine father images in several contemporary myths of the ancient Near East. Three mythologies in particular outside the Bible stand out as characteristic of religious imagination in that region during this period: the Babylonian creation story, Enuma Elis, the Canaanite Baal poems from Ugarit, and the Egyptian tale of Osiris and Isis. After reviewing each of these briefly, I will turn to the biblical myth and then conclude with a few thoughts regarding the significance of the comparisons that emerge.

## Enuma Elis

Religion in second millennium B.C.E. Mesopotamia was characterized by a large number of nature deities thought to be organized into a divine state. They are also represented in the myths as a divine family, the dynamics of which are most fully revealed in the Babylonian creation story, *Enuma Elis*.[5]

Two crises marked the coming into being of the world as we know it, according to this myth, both precipitated in part by conduct attributed to fathers. At the beginning of creation, the *Enuma Elis* tells us, there existed only commingling salt and fresh waters, conceived of as two parental deities, Tiamat, the mother, and Apsu, the father (I, 1–5). In their midst the younger gods were born: Lahmu and Lahamu, Anshar and Kishar (silt-gods), Anu (the sky-god), and the earth-god Nudimmud or Ea (I, 6–20). The birth of these children, however, brought little joy to their parents, for they were boisterous and loud and disturbed their sleep, so much so that something had to be done. And it was father Apsu, we are told, who hit upon a bold idea. The children should be killed (I,

20–40)! Mother Tiamat, however, upon hearing of this solution, was, to say the least, less than enthusiastic and pleaded with her husband to have patience (I, 40–43). Father Apsu, however, was in no mood to be dissuaded. His face "radiant" (the text says), he set about executing his murderous plan. But before he could accomplish it, word of his intentions came to his son Ea, who promptly cast a spell over him, putting him to sleep (I, 64). He then proceeded to divest his father of the emblems of his authority (band, tiara, halo), bound him and murdered him (I, 69), after which he built himself a chamber in the midst of the corpse (I, 71–77). Thus the curtain is drawn on Act I of the *Enuma Elis.*

Needless to say the drama to this point has portrayed a family in considerable disarray. The father especially is characterized as a brutish figure at odds with his wife and irritated by his children to the point of wanting to kill them. The children survive by murdering him instead. Thus were the foundations laid for our cosmic home!

A second chapter in the drama of creation begins when Ea, fresh from murdering his father, marries and has a son of his own, the storm-god Marduk (I, 79–84). With Marduk's entry into the story a contest begins to take shape between two groups of gods, those in league with mother Tiamat, now a widow, and those associated with the younger generation of gods under the leadership of Anshar. Mother Tiamat, it turns out, in the aftermath of her husband's death, was persuaded to do what she had earlier pleaded with him not to do: murder her children (I, 111–117). With this in mind she began fashioning an army of monsters and elevated one of them, Kingu, as commander in chief (I, 125–161).

The crisis that now unfolds is portrayed in the myth as the most severe in the entire history of cosmogenesis (II, 1–48). Who is going to stop mother Tiamat from attacking and destroying her own children and with them the world-home they have succeeded in creating for themselves? The sky-god Anshar, himself now an exalted father deity (Apsu being dead), would appear to be the logical candidate. But Anshar, we are told, upon hearing of the frightful things mother Tiamat was planning to do, shrank back in fear (II, 50) and turned for assistance to two father deities next in rank, Anu and Ea. But they too were as fearful as he (II, 53–87).

Collectively helpless, the divine elders summoned an assembly of the gods, and there it was that the solution to this crisis was arrived at

(II, 88–99). What the fathers were too frightened to do, individually or collectively, was laid on the shoulders of the youthful Marduk, and he responded magnificently, it is said, but only after shrewdly exacting a pledge that he would reign as king of the universe in his father's place (II, 122–129). Then without anyone's help he faced the terrible Tiamat, distended and destroyed her, and fashioned the universe out of the remains of her body (IV, 90–145). The myth closes with Marduk completing creation (V–VI, 44) and being given a temple at which were recited his fifty glorious names (VI, 45–VII, 144).

It is not fathers then who rule the universe in the Babylonian vision of reality, but sons, and they rule not with them, but in spite of them. Fathers, it is implied, can be cruel and weak. Sons must defend themselves against them and rise above them. Mothers also can be harsh and destructive and bring terror to both fathers and sons. Then too sons must be resourceful and courageous and not expect their fathers to help them. From this myth we might conjecture that Mesopotamian society was characterized by ambitious, bellicose sons and weak fathers—a configuration, interestingly enough, that recurs in the *Gilgamesh Epic*, a popular Mesopotamian narrative roughly contemporary in time with the *Enuma Elis*. In it we read of the journey to maturity of a famous king. His growing up, it turns out, was exceptionally long and tortuous for the very reason that in his case too the fathers were frightened and weak and unable to discipline or guide him, so that he had to find his way pretty much on his own, through trial and error, except for the help of a peer.[6]

## The Baal Myths

Our picture of second millennium Canaanite mythology has been significantly enhanced through the discovery of tablets in the library of the chief priest of the storm god Baal in the ancient city of Ugarit, among which are several that relate Baal's ascent to divine kingship.[7] Baal's father El is creator and titular ruler of the universe. In reality, like the father gods of Mesopotamia, El plays a peculiarly weak and inept role in the life of the world. Three episodes in particular bring this out.

In what is generally regarded as one of the major episodes of the opening drama of this myth the gods are shown assembling at the home of El in the far north (III AB B). Baal is standing at his father's side when messengers arrive from Yam-Nahar (Sea-River) demanding of the assembly and of El that Baal be handed over to them. Apparently they wish to destroy him and inundate the land over which he presides. Their challenge is thus a similar one to that posed by Tiamat in the Enuma Elis. In this instance, however, Sea-River is not thought of as the primeval mother, but as another son in the family of El. In any case, El and his assembly appear to be just as powerless to deal with the challenge as were their Mesopotamian counterparts. To our surprise, in fact, El accedes to the wishes of Yam-Nahar (either out of fear or because he favored Yam-Nahar in the first place). But Baal is quite prepared to take matters into his own hands. Ignoring his father, with the help of a divine craftsman, he sets about clubbing Yam-Nahar into submission (III AB A). In this myth the son not only rises above the weak father to rule the world (as in Mesopotamia), but does so in the face of his father's pathetic willingness to let him be destroyed.

There follows the story of how, in the aftermath of this deed, Baal managed to obtain for himself a palace (II, AB; V AB). In Mesopotamia Marduk was gladly given a house by the divine fathers in recognition of his deeds on their behalf. In the Canaanite myth Baal's destruction of Yam-Nahar initially went unrecognized by his father. As it turns out father El had to be browbeaten into allowing his son to have a house of his own. The goddess Anath, Baal's sister, plays a particularly important role in this part of the drama. When she learns that her brother, in spite of his victory over Sea-River (Yam-Nahar), is still living at home and without a house of his own, she is furious and threatens to bloody her father's grey hair if he doesn't do something (V AB E, 6–14).

A kind of crescendo in the Baal stories is reached in a final episode where yet another member of this divine family is introduced, one whose destructive fury no one, apparently, not even Baal, can tame or control. This is El's son Mot (death) who, "one lip to earth and one to heaven" (I AB ii, 1), swallows him, thereby consigning him to the netherworld. In the face of this tragedy father El is portrayed as particularly helpless and distraught. Earlier he was ready enough to let Baal be taken captive by Yam-Nahar. But now that Baal is actually dead, he descends from his throne, throws himself into the dust and covers his loins with sackcloth (I AB vi). Salvation comes not from him, but again from Baal's sister Anath who somehow rescues him from Mot's jaws.

Thus in Canaanite mythology as in Mesopotamia, it is not the father but the son (and in this instance also his sister) who creates the conditions necessary for a tolerable existence in this dangerous universe. And more often than not, they do this not with the father's blessing and help, but either in opposition to him, or in the face of his pathetic weakness. Fathers head up the cosmic home, these myths seem to be saying. They can even be kindly at times and emotionally involved in what is happening around them. But for the most part they are mere figureheads, not the ones really in charge.

## Osiris and Isis

Basic clues to the dynamics at work in Egyptian life and religion can also be found in myths that functioned paradigmatically throughout Egyptian history. The most important of these, strangely enough, are nowhere to be found in their entirety in extant Egyptian literature. For their preservation we are indebted to the Greek historian Plutarch who lived in the first century C.E. and pieced them together from written and oral traditions available to him at that time.[8] They concern the Egyptian parental deities Isis (mother) and Osiris (father). The stories begin by telling of the benevolent rule of father Osiris over Egypt by means of which he was able to bring widespread peace and prosperity. He then set about carrying his teachings to the rest of the world. During his absence his sister-wife Isis ruled Egypt in his place.

A dark turning point in the story occurred, however, upon his return when a banquet was held in his honor to which his brother Set, along with others, had been invited. During the banquet a coffin was brought into the hall and Osiris was tricked into lying in it. When he did so, Set and those with him rose up and put a lid on the box, took it from the banquet hall and floated it down the Nile River. This might have been the end of the story, were it not for the reaction of Isis. Briefly summarized, she set off in search of her husband's corpse, eventually found it, brought it back to Egypt and conceived a son, Horus, by it. Once again, however, the wicked Set entered the picture. Having learned of the return of his brother's corpse, he stole it and, after chopping it into fourteen pieces, scattered them all over Egypt. Isis, however, rescued her husband a second time and now by means of magical rites and incantations succeeded in restoring him to life in the afterworld. There, the Egyptians believed, Osiris continued to reign, his benevolent image, in the course of time, merging with that of the solar deity Re (sun). A final chapter of the myth relates how Osiris commissioned and empowered his son, Horus, to avenge his murder. This Horus subsequently did in several bloody battles in which Set was roundly defeated and destroyed.

Unique to this myth, in comparison to the Mesopotamian and Canaanite stories we have just reviewed, is the degree to which there is present here a powerful, wise father who brought peace to Egypt and in doing so succeeded as well in winning the loyalty and respect of wife and son. But here too the image of the father is a flawed one. How easily Osiris was outwitted by his wicked brother! He would appear to be naive. As a consequence his wife and son were compelled to play excessively demanding roles on his behalf. True, in Egyptian imagination Osiris was the ultimate power who ruled the universe from his home in eternity, but the stories declared that his very existence there was due to the saving action of his wife, and it was his son finally who had to rule on earth and vindicate his name. In Egypt too, as in Mesopotamia and Canaan, a son, and in this instance also his mother, are the ultimate guarantors of the triumph of life over death.[9]

# The Bible

The Bible has no stories to tell about its god comparable to those we have just surveyed. And yet it would be misleading to say that it has no myths. Rather here there has occurred "a reorientation of the locale of myth," as John Priest has put it.[10] Instead of interacting with other gods the biblical God is portrayed in his relations with an historical people,

Israel. Thus "the history of Israel is the biography" of its god and "the mode of the Israelite expression of myth."[11]

Three characteristics of the god so revealed are highlighted in almost all the stories about him. There is first of all the fact that he is "he" (and not "she").[12] This "he," of course, is a divine father (Dt 32:6; Jer 3:19; Is 63:16; Mal 2:10; Lk 11:2 Eph 3:14f.), not a son, and one who in some sense is like the god of the fathers (Ex 3:15) and "El," the father of the gods (Gn 33:20; Jos 22:22).[13]

Contrasting sharply, however, with every other father deity we have looked at so far is his insistence, secondly, that those who serve him shall serve him exclusively and alone (Ex 20:3; Dt 5:7). This unique attribute is explained in several texts as resulting from his "jealousy" (Ex 20:5; Dt 5:9; 32:16; Jos 24:19; Nm 25:11). In one text his very name is said to be "the jealous one" for, it adds, "a jealous god *(el)* is he" (Ex 34:14).[14] Being father (and not mother), this jealousy must be understood, first of all, as paternal jealousy directed against competing mother, son and daughter deities for the right to primacy in his own family. In other words, in biblical myth a divine father has divested himself, so to speak, of the cowardice and passivity so often attributed to fathers in extra-biblical myth and is viewed as taking charge of the affairs of his household (Ex 4:22b–23).

The very name of this god, Yahweh, may itself be symbolic of this remarkable transformation. It is quite likely a third person singular (masculine) causative form of the verb "to be" ("he causes to be") and there are reasons to think that originally it may have been used in conjunction with *el* (god), as in Psalm 10:12, with the meaning: "*el* causes to be."[15] To the question what god (or *el*) causes to be, Parke-Taylor has argued that it is his own people.[16] This in any case is the answer implied by Psalm 100, Isaiah 43:1 and Deuteronomy 32:6, the latter of which asks: "Is this not your father [Yahweh], who gave you being, who made you, by whom you subsist?" Yahweh then is a divine father, but, unlike his paternal contemporaries, a uniquely active one ("he causes to be"). In his zeal (jealousy) he created a people among whom he lives as the sole guiding force.

A third characteristic of this god is his goodness. This was unforgettably demonstrated by the very way he created a people in the first place: his liberating them from slavery (Ex 15) and his gracious covenant involving stipulations (Ex 20), all of which were seen to be for the well-being of the community (Ps 15:7–11). But this was also the essence of what was revealed concerning him in a remarkable audition that occurred in the aftermath of these events. To Moses' request for a glimpse of his "glory" (Ex 33:18), Yahweh passed before him and proclaimed, "Yahweh, Yahweh, God *[el]* of tenderness and compassion, slow to anger, rich in faithful love and constancy…" (Ex 34:6f.).[17]

This by and large (with now this, now that feature emphasized) is the portrait of God that we encounter throughout the biblical story, Old and New Testaments. There is one God and one God only to be worshiped and served. He is a divine father, yet not cowardly or withdrawn like so many of his paternal contemporaries, but alert rather, vigorously involved and uniformly just, kind and compassionate. "After all, you are our Father…you, Yahweh, are our Father, 'Our Redeemer' is your name from of old" (Is 63:16). "Our Father, who art in heaven, hallowed be thy name" (Mt 6:9).

Only here in the myths of the ancient Near East is it said that a father-god, worthy of being hallowed, is fully in charge of the cosmic home.

## Concluding Comments

The main purpose of this essay, as previously stated, has been to highlight the contrasts that emerge when the divine father in biblical myth is compared with father divinities in several contemporary ancient Near Eastern mythologies. Such a comparison, as noted, raises questions about the assumption that biblical father religion is simply continuous with wider ancient Near Eastern patriarchalism. It would appear to be more accurate to say, as does David Bakan, that the Bible registers an important socio-religious shift, one in which, on the human level, men began assuming a larger role in the care of their families.[18] That men will do this, or do it well, history teaches, cannot be taken for granted. A "crisis of paternalization," as Bakan terms it, is not only associated with certain periods in history; it is one that is repeated in the individual life histories of many males who become fathers, generation after generation.[19] And in this may lie, in part at least, the relevance of the Bible right down to the present. Its firm belief in God as effectively caring father undergirds and encourages human fathers in the taking on of caretaking roles. In the light of what we now know about the importance of fathering for the emotional well-being of children, this may be viewed in itself as a not inconsiderable contribution to the life of the world.[20]

# 5.

# DEPATRIARCHALIZING GOD IN BIBLICAL INTERPRETATION: A CRITIQUE

*The proposal that God is sometimes thought of as feminine or genderless in biblical tradition is not supported by the evidence. On the other hand, Yahweh is not simply regarded as male either, but as a father whose caring is often experienced as mother-like in its tenderness and compassion.*

In an innovative essay entitled "Depatriarchalizing in Biblical Interpretation," Phyllis Trible sounded a theme that has become increasingly powerful in modern biblical study.[1] While biblical religion is clearly patriarchal, she wrote, not a few biblical texts point beyond patriarchy to a more egalitarian ideal in human relations.[2] Indeed, she argued, a "depatriarchalizing principle" is at work in scripture which, once recognized, permits us "to translate biblical faith without sexism" on the authority of the biblical tradition itself.[3]

In this essay I will be focusing exclusively on the way Trible and others, in following through on this project, go about "depatriarchalizing" the biblical representation of *God*. Their point of view in summary is this:

(1) Biblical references to God as patriarch or father…are sexist, in that maleness…is thereby divinized and men are encourage to think of themselves as godlike in ways women cannot.

(2) Yet as a matter of fact a patriarchal or masculine representation of God is not nearly as predominant in the Bible as generally thought. Indeed there are biblical texts that either deny that God is male, or portray him as female, or as above and beyond gender altogether.

(3) Consequently, biblical tradition itself can be said to temper and rel ativize the sexist patriarchal notion of God to be found there in many passages.

So far as I know these novel ideas, which are already enshrined in Trible's essay on "God" in the *Interpreter's Dictionary of the Bible, Supplementary Volume,* have to date not been seriously questioned.[4] And yet, as I hope to indicate, the evidence cited thus far in their support is far from cogent.

In the critique that follows I will be focusing for the most part on the second of the two points referred to above: that there are texts in the Bible that either deny that God is male or portray him as female or as above and beyond gender altogether. But to avoid misunderstanding as to what my motives are in making this critique, I will begin with a few comments regarding the first and third points as well: that the biblical representation of God as father is a sexist notion that needs to be tempered and relativized.

## Is the Representation of God as Father, as such, a Sexist Notion?

There appears to be an unexamined assumption in the writings of Trible and others that biblical "patriarchy" has to do quite simply with male supremacy and that this is demeaning for women. If God is male, the argument goes, then male is God and it follows that whenever God is represented as male-patriarch, females are prejudicially denigrated and males favored.[5] But is this analysis adequate?

As some indication that it is not, it should be noted that the term "patriarch" refers not to males as such, but to a quite specific male role: that of "pater" or father. Hence, to refer to Yahweh simply as male is to misconstrue the issue. Moreover, the "supremacy" of males in that role (if such it is) is one that has an impact for good or ill not only on females, but on males also, for men as fathers, together with their wives, exercise responsibility for the care of children of both sexes. This suggests that for an appreciation of "pater" as divine metaphor we must attend to the complex dynamics of fathering in the nurture of children and not just to the issue of male supremacy as it affects women.

Those who have done this stress that for an adequate understanding of the significance of the father-role some awareness is needed, first of all, of the strength of the bond that typically exists between *mothers* and children by virtue of their symbiotic tie during pregnancy, birth and nursing.[6] It is this biologically determined relationship, so essential in laying the foundations of healthy development, that shapes those qualities usually associated with mothering: unconditional availability, receptivity and tenderness. Fathers, on the other hand, when effectively present to their families, insert themselves into the bond between mother and child as a "second other" by an initiative very much like that of adoption. Where this initiative is energetic and winsome, developmental psychology teaches us, an essential autonomy from the mother is fostered and children of both sexes are significantly helped in orienting themselves to the cultural universe outside the home with its laws and ethical norms. Maternal values are not thereby repudiated—fathers too may embody tender mother-like attributes without ceasing to be fathers—but the exclusivity of the mother-bond is challenged by an authority that separates the child and orients it toward its personal future in extra-familial society.[7]

Seen in this light, the metaphor "father," when used of God, is far from being simply a symbol of masculine dominance or privilege. It may in fact embrace feminine or maternal attributes, but in combination with what Vergote terms "firmness and directive action."[8] If the father symbolizes God better than the mother," he adds, "it is thus because of that which paternal law effects in the family triangle."[9]

In arguing then, as I will in the following section, that the biblical representation of God is more, not less patriarchal than generally recognized and that the texts cited to the contrary do not say what they are said to be saying by Trible and others, I trust I will not be misunderstood as favoring the denigration of women. On the contrary there are solid reasons for thinking that the biblical representation of God as caring father has had a generally humanizing effect in the lives of both men and women.[10]

## Does the Bible Itself Depatriarchalize God?

The data that Trible and others appeal to as evidence of depatriarchalizing God in the Bible may be classified in a threefold manner:

(1) texts ascribing feminine activities or emotions to God;
(2) terms used to characterize God whose root meanings are feminine;
(3) texts explicitly stating that God is not male, hence intimating that God is beyond gender altogether.

This third groups of texts, I suggest, merits our attention first of all, for were it true, as Trible has put it, that they intimate that "Israel was quite aware that a masculine label for Deity is dangerous"[11] and that hence "all analogies to the freedom and transcendence of God are inadequate,"[12] then this might have implications for the way the additional evidence for depatriarchalizing God referred to above is to be understood.

But are there in fact biblical texts that point to a God beyond gender?

It may be noted to begin with that the passages cited in support of this thesis are very few in number—three to be exact: Numbers 23:19; 1 Samuel 15:29; Hosea 11:9. Considering the size of the biblical canon, this in itself is remarkable. Here and nowhere else is there even an inkling of such an idea. Furthermore, a comparison of the three texts quickly indicates that two of them, Numbers 23:19 and 1 Samuel 15:29, are virtually identical, and the third, Hosea 11:9, is quite similar to the other two.

But do even these three texts say what Trible suggests they say? Both Numbers 23:19 and 1 Samuel 15:29 declare that "God is not man (*'îš* )" in the specific sense that he does not lie. The contrast then is *not* between a God beyond gender and "man" as male. In fact such a contrast is excluded by the second line in both texts which states that neither is God *'ādām* (1 Sam 15:29) or *ben 'ādām* (Nm 23:19) "that he should repent." *'Ādām* is the Hebrew term for "human being" inclusive of both sexes (Gn 1:31). Hosea 11:9 differs from the other two texts only in the sense that there God himself says: "For I am God and not *'îš*," and specifies as the point of contrast, not that he does not lie, but that he ("the holy one in your midst") is full of compassion.

These texts then are quite specific as to the point of the contrast between God and man and quite deliberate in clarifying that by *'îš* is meant not "male" but *'ādām* (human being). Furthermore, in all three texts "God" is referred to as *'ēl*, a general term for deity, but also the name of the Canaanite father deity. In Numbers 23:19 it is said of this *'ēl*: "has he spoken and shall he not do it, has he uttered his word and shall he not make good?" In short, the deity referred to here is clearly identified as masculine-paternal. How then can it be argued on the basis of these texts that a "masculine label" for deity was thought to be dangerous or that a depatriarchalizing principle was at work in biblical religion?

But if it is misleading to suggest that biblical authors ever thought of God as above or beyond gender, are there not certain texts that "temper" the dominance of the masculine-patriarchal image of God thereby suggesting that he could, on occasion at least, be thought of as female or mother?

As noted, two types of evidence have been put forward in defense of this thesis:

- texts, first of all, which purportedly ascribe feminine characteristics or emotions to God;
- terms characterizing God whose root meanings are feminine.

In this latter category are two terms in particular: the Hebrew adjective *raḥûm* (meaning "compassion"), which Trible points out is based on the Hebrew root *reḥem* (meaning "womb"), and *Šadday* which Trible, following Cross, believes originally meant "breasts."[13] "Used only of deity," Trible writes, "*raḥûm* is not language for a father who creates by begetting but for a mother who creates by nourishing in the womb."[14] Bearing this in mind, Trible translates the verb *rāḥam* as "mother compassion" in Jeremiah 31:20 where God is quoted as saying of Ephraim: "For as often as I speak of him, I do remember him still. Therefore my inner parts yearn for him; I will surely have mother compassion on him...."[15]

Were this translation correct, why would it be inappropriate for Yahweh as father to say that he yearns for his children with motherly compassion? Cannot fathers also experience "motherly compassion"? As a matter of fact *raḥûm* occurs frequently in Canaanite texts as a characterization of the Canaanite father deity *'Ēl*, and in Psalm 103:13, as Trible herself has noted,[16] it is said quite explicitly that "as a father pities [or has compassion for] his children, so Yahweh pities [or has compassion for] those who fear him."[17]

Clearly, then, in the ancient Near East at least, fathers, human and divine, were readily characterized as having compassion. Needless to say, root meanings of words do not necessarily determine subsequent usages, a point that applies as well to Trible's suggestion that in Genesis 49:25 "the God of thy father" is balanced by a maternal image implicit in the name *Šadday*, because of its possible root meaning "breasts" and the occurrence of the word "breasts" *(šādaym)* at the verse's end. Even were this etymology correct (a derivation from a root word meaning "field" has also been defended),[18] its secondary meaning, Cross notes, was evidently "mountain,"[19] the abode of *'Ēl* in Canaanite mythology. It is once again difficult to see how an argument for the existence of a depatriarchalizing principle in biblical tradition can be made on such a basis.

We are left then, as evidence of depatriarchalizing tendencies in the Bible, with those passages where it is intimated that God acts in maternal or feminine ways or has feminine qualities or emotions. Examples would be: Genesis 1:26–27, where both male and female are said to have been created in the image and likeness of God; Psalm 22:9–10, where Yahweh is likened to a midwife; Deuteronomy 32:18, where he is referred to as "the God who gave you birth"; Numbers 11:12, where Moses asks "Have I given birth to this people?"—alluding, it is suggested, to the fact that it is God who like a mother really gave birth to

Israel; Isaiah 42:14a, where God calls out like a woman in travail; Isaiah 49:15, where God says that even if a mother forgets her baby at the breast, "I will not forget" (thus likening himself to a mother); Isaiah 66:9, where God is characterized as the one who brings to birth and comforts Jerusalem as a mother comforts a child; Psalm 131:2, where the psalmist declares that his soul is quieted before God, like a child quieted at its mother's breast (implying thereby that God is like a mother to him).

There can be no doubt that these and several other texts that might perhaps be added to this list[20] do attribute mother-like or feminine actions and attributes to God. The point at issue is whether in doing so God is actually thought of *as* mother (and not just mother-*like*). This is excluded by the fact that the texts in question clearly and consistently maintain a paternal-masculine point of reference. Not once in the Bible is God addressed as mother, said to be mother, or referred to with feminine pronouns. On the contrary, gender usage throughout clearly specifies that the root metaphor is masculine-father.

Psalm 22:9–10 is a case in point. Concerning this text Trible has written: "Deity" is here portrayed as "both midwife and mother. She [sic] takes the infant from the womb and places it safely upon maternal breasts; in turn she becomes the very one upon whom the child is cast from birth."[21] But the text itself nowhere refers to God as "she." Psalm 22:9 is a prayer which opens and closes with in invocative "you" which in Hebrew has a masculine form *('attâ )* and a feminine form *( 'att)*. In his prayer the psalmist uses the masculine "you" *('attâ)*, as one would expect of a worshiper addressing Yahweh: "It was you [masculine]," he prays, "who drew me from the womb, and soothed me on my mother's breasts; on you was I cast from my birth, from the womb I have belonged to you [masculine]."

It is clearly not true then that the psalmist in this passage is actually thinking of Yahweh *as* midwife or mother. Rather *like* a gentle midwife, he says, you, Yahweh, have been my guardian from the moment of my birth. Here as throughout the Hebrew Bible Yahweh is portrayed as a caring, resourceful father. Genesis 1:26–27 (cited by Trible as a "topical clue" in her most ambitious work on this subject)[22] is no exception. After declaring "Let us make man *( 'adam )* in our image…" the text specifies, "So God created man [male and female] in *his* image…" (Gn 1:27).

Apparently biblical authors saw no incongruity in characterizing both men and women as bearing the image and likeness of a paternal deity.

## Summary and Conclusions

In her initial essay calling for depatriarchalizing in biblical interpretation Trible concluded that modern assertions that God is masculine, even when they are qualified, are misleading and detrimental if not altogether inaccurate, for "unlike fertility gods, Yahweh is neither male nor female; neither he nor she."[23] In this essay I too have tried to indicate that referring to Yahweh simply as male is to misconstrue the issues. Already at its point of origins biblical Yahwism sought to differentiate itself not only from the worship of feminine deities but alternative masculine deities as well (Baal, for example, the Canaanite son-deity). On the other hand it had no hesitation confessing that a continuity existed between Yahweh and the Canaanite father deity El ("El of gods is Yahweh"—Jos 22:22).[24]

Yahweh then is not simply male, but father to his worshipers[25] as the name Yahweh itself may imply ("he causes to be").[26] True, Yahweh as father is pictured occasionally as acting with a tenderness and care that is mother-like. But nowhere is it ever said or suggested that he *is* mother. According to Jesus his very "name" is father and the hallowing of that name is the focal point of religious devotion.[27] "The God of Judaism is undoubtedly a father-symbol and father image," Raphael Patai has written, "possibly the greatest such symbol and image conceived by man. Nor," he adds, "can there be any doubt as to the psychological need answered by this image. This, together with the great moral imperatives, was the unique contribution of prophetic Judaism to mankind."[28]

# PART THREE
# HUMAN FATHERING IN
# BIBLICAL TRADITION

*We can hardly open the Bible without finding some allusion to the biological connectedness between male progenitors and their offspring...*

*The Bible may be interpreted as a document representing the crisis of paternalization, all the changes involved in the male's assumption of the various obligations of fatherhood.\**

*David Bakan, *And They Took Themselves Wives, The Emergence of Patriarchy in Western Civilization* (New York: Harper & Row, 1979), p. 12f.

# 6.

# NEW MODES OF HUMAN FATHERING (HEBREW SCRIPTURES)

*Through the rituals of redemption of the first-born, circumcision, and Passover faith in God as redemptive, caring father was linked to human fathering and Israelite fathers came to be involved in the care and teaching of their own children to a degree that was unique in the world of their time.*

In this essay I want to indicate how in connection with the revelation of God as father in biblical tradition there emerged in Israel a new appreciation for the role and function of a certain kind of human fathering, and how new modes of fathering actually did come into existence in this context. I want to be careful not to overstate my case in this regard. I am not referring to a sudden, radical change whereby Israelite fathers became ideal fathers. I do not know, if we had the means for measuring this, whether overall during the centuries when the Hebrew Bible was coming into existence, Israelite fathers would stand out as all that different from their counterparts in other cultures. What I am suggesting is that under the influence of their experience of God as caring, redemptive father (Is 63:16), especially from the days of Moses and Israel's exodus from Egypt onward (Dt 32:6), innovations in fathering were introduced that over the centuries did serve to consolidate and strengthen the role of men as fathers in their families to a degree unknown elsewhere in the ancient world.[1]

The chief heir and custodian of these biblical innovations in fathering in the modern world are the Jews, since Christians, even though also regarding Hebrew scripture as part of their scriptures, have by and large ignored those texts that prescribe for the new modes of fathering I am going to be discussing. In fact, it might be said that a critical distinction between Judaism and Christianity arises right at this point. Whereas Judaism has both continued and elaborated the father-family traditions enshrined in Hebrew scripture, Christianity has to some considerable extent relaxed or ignored these traditions. I will be saying more about *this* issue elsewhere (see Chapters 7 and 11). Here, I will be concentrating on identifying and explaining the innovations themselves.

There are two types of data especially I will be looking at in this regard. There are, to begin with, certain *rituals* or liturgies that merit careful study—rites in which fathers play the leading roles, and which, I hope to show, reveal certain new trends in fathering. And then I will be looking at evidence that points to the emergence of a unique sense of responsibility among Israelite fathers for being the *teachers* of their children.

There is a third set of data bearing on fathering in Israel the importance of which needs to be recognized and acknowledged, even though I will not be discussing it in any detail. I refer to the way biblical tradition upholds the integrity and importance of the marital bond between a man and his wife by its portrayal of the complementary nature of this relationship in its normative creation stories (Gn 2) and by its very explicit and detailed teaching against adultery in all of its forms— whether as incest (see Lv 18; 20:8–21), or philandering (see Prv 5; 7:6–27), or as the outright seduction of another man's wife (Ex 20:14). Needless to say, where adultery is *not* proscribed in this outright manner, the foundations of the father-involved family are severely undermined. Israel was therefore not unjustified in regarding its laws and teachings on this particular set of issues as among its most important distinguishing characteristics. Failure to hold firm on this point, it was believed, would result in its being "vomited out" of its land (Lv 18:24, 28). Marital fidelity, on the other hand, guaranteed the stability of the two-parent family and helped to secure the respect due to both parents, father and mother.[2]

# Father-Family Rituals

Too little attention has been paid in the study of the Hebrew Bible, by Christians especially, to the rituals prescribed there. It is these, very often, that are the keys to an understanding of the structures of faith that were predominant. As "little dramas" repeatedly enacted, rituals embody and communicate to successive generations the world outlook of those who perform them—what they believe to be important.

When we do take note of this point, one soon becomes aware of the striking fact that among the most important biblical rituals are several having to do with the family, and with the *father's* role in the family in particular. It can then also be readily observed that the editors of the Bible have preserved the records of these particular rituals in Exodus 12 and 13, right in the midst of their narrative accounts of Israel's foundational experience of exodus and liberation from Egypt. Obviously, their purpose in doing so was to communicate their conviction that it would be precisely by means of the enactment of these rituals in particular that the memory and significance of Israel's experience with God at this foundational juncture of its existence could best be kept alive.

The actions or rituals alluded to in these chapters are threefold:

- Passover (here combined with the festival of unleavened bread)— 12:1–28; 13:3–10;
- redemption of the first-born (12:43–51; 13:1–2; 13:11–16;
- circumcision—this latter being more presupposed than com manded in the instructions of this section (12:48–51).

# The Rituals as a Group

Before examining these rituals individually and trying to ascertain their significance, I would like to try to characterize them as a group. And the first thing I want to emphasize is that each of them is in fact a ritual, a little drama, a sacred drama, and that such dramas are hereby given a central place in the life of the biblical community. Biblical faith is not so

much taught as caught, not so much transmitted (from generation to generation) through formal teachings as by means of symbolic actions.

But just as noteworthy is the fact, secondly, that these rituals are
rites of the *family* (as just suggested)—and of the *nuclear* family
specifically—not rites of the sanctuary or of the community as a whole.
In other words, these oldest and most enduring religious ceremonies
are *nuclear family* affairs (that is, actions of the household of father,
mother, children, servants and guests resident in, or attached to, this
primary unit).*

Furthermore, and equally important, I suggest (and this point too is not
usually sufficiently noted or emphasized), they are family rituals in which
the father plays the leading role.

Finally, all of these father-family rituals have to do above all with the
father's role as caretaker and guardian of his *children*. Hence, they may be
characterized as father-family rituals in which the father is called upon to
perform or do certain actions bearing upon the well-being of his progeny.

Let us look now more closely at each of these rituals in this light.

## Redemption of the First Born

I will begin our survey with what might well have been the oldest of these
ritual actions: the redemption of the first-born. In the background is the
widespread practice of ritually slaughtering a first-born as an act of piety
and devotion to God (as dramatized in the near slaughter of Isaac by his
father Abraham in Genesis 22). The shape of the exodus narrative as a
whole seems to reflect the background presence of this gruesome ritual.[3]
In the story of the plagues, for example, emphasis is placed on the fact
that the tenth and most devastating of these, the one that set the stage for
Israel's liberation from Egypt, was the slaughter of the *Egyptian* male
firstborn (Ex 12:21–34). This theme surfaces again in Exodus 13:1 in the
commandment that *all* first-born, "the first birth from every
womb…whether man or beast…" shall be consecrated to Yahweh (com-
pare Ex 22:28–29), and then again in the ritual alluded to in 13:11–16, the
one that declares that an exception shall be made in the case of first-born

sons. They, it is specified, shall be "redeemed" by offering in their stead an animal sacrifice (13:13).

Given this cultural background, the ritual of "the redemption of the first-born" must have been experienced as a most impressive one regarding which a first-born son, upon growing up, might indeed have remarked to his father (as it says he would, in Exodus 13:14), "What does this mean?"—to which the father was instructed to reply that this is a "sign on your hand" by which the memory will be kept alive that "by the strength of his hand Yahweh brought us out of Egypt" (13:16).

In other words, through this ritual the hard-won insight (already embodied in the story of Abraham's near sacrifice of his first-born)[4] that God wants their devotion, not that fathers kill their sons, was brought to dramatic, confessional expression—here, however, within the framework of the story of Israel's liberation from Egypt. Just as the tragic death of Egypt's first-born was ritually alluded to in the offering up of the first-born of the flocks, so the memory of the redemptive preservation of *Israel's* first-born during the same sequence of events was kept alive by the rite of the son's release. In this way the truth was dramatized that Israel's God is a "redemptive father" (Is 63:16) whom Israelite fathers should emulate in their care of the children given to them.

The spiritual dynamic embodied in this ritual can be sensed in the way it is still being enacted among Jews right down to the present.[5] As currently practiced, the redemption of a first-born son occurs on the child's thirty-first day of life, when it is more or less certain that the child will live. He is then brought by his father (in the presence of invited guests) to the rabbi in charge of a given synagogue. Instead of an animal sacrifice as substitute for the son, a coin, minted specifically for this ritual, is brought as the redemption offering.

As the father approaches the rabbi with his child, he is asked whether he wishes to redeem his child or leave him at the altar! The father in reply expresses his desire to redeem and keep his son, hands over the redemption money as a substitute, and then recites two benedictions: one for the fulfillment of the commandment of redemption and another a prayer of thanks. The rabbi then solemnly pronounces three times: "Your son is redeemed, your son is redeemed, your son is redeemed," after which he returns the child to his father.

The emotional impact that a ritual of this kind might have had (and has) on a father is only too obvious. Through it he is compelled to face up to the prospect of getting rid of his son, and he must make explicit and public his decision to redeem and keep him instead. He thereby pledges himself in the sight of God and his community to take ownership of this child—to keep and care for him—and gives voice to his gratitude for the privilege of being able to do so.

The son on his part grows to maturity knowing that he was redeemed by his father in this manner—knowing that he was wanted, chosen and loved by his father as an infant in a very deliberate, self-conscious way. This act, linked as it is to Yahweh's redemption of Israel, was simultaneously an expression of religious faith and commitment. To redeem and care for children in this manner was spiritually motivated; since this was what Yahweh himself had done in redeeming *his* children from Egypt, this is what human fathers can be expected to do with their children as well.

The way this ritual has served through the centuries to consolidate paternal identities and cement the bonds between fathers and children in the community of those who practiced it should be evident.

## Circumcision

But there was yet another father-ritual that made an even more important contribution to this same end, and this is the rite of circumcision. Its importance lies in part in the fact that this particular ritual was (and is) performed not just once in the life of a family, at the birth of a first-born son, but repeatedly in conjunction with the birth of every male child. Furthermore, the ritual action called for is more traumatic in some respects than the one enacted during the redemption of the first-born, for in this instance the father must wound his son in a manner that is painful and leaves a permanent mark on his body.

Circumcision refers to the removal of the foreskin of the male penis. The resulting wound is of course, generally speaking, a minor one, leaving the individual involved none the worse for it. As such it may be described as a "symbolic wound," for its significance lies not in the surgery itself so much as in what the surgery symbolizes—in the thoughts and emotions surrounding this action.

What were those? Since the biblical texts describing this ritual are rather vague on this point, it may be useful to look, first of all, at the meaning this ritual has had (and still has) in other cultural settings.[6] Among most extra-biblical peoples (the contemporary Muslim Arabs would be an example) circumcision functions as a puberty ritual marking the transition of young boys to adulthood. Felix Bryk, after a thorough review of the subject, sides with those who view it as having originated in the belief (possibly correct) that it increases male procreative power.[7] Thus, in most extra-biblical cultures it was (and is) regarded as a mark of manhood which is to be inscribed on the flesh *at puberty* preparatory to marriage. In Israel too this close association of circumcision with puberty and marriage is preserved in the Hebrew terms for "bridegroom," "son-in-law" and "father-in-law," all of which are derived from the single Hebrew root which even today yet, in Arabic, means "to circumcise."[8]

However, viewed against this background, what is striking about the biblical circumcision ritual is the fact that here it was *not* performed at *puberty* (although there are passing references to this form of the ritual in the brief notice in Genesis 17:23 that Abraham circumcised his son Ishmael *when he was thirteen*). Nor was it carried out as a ritual of the community (although again there are hints of this custom as well; see Jos 5:2–9; Gn 34:13–19). Within biblical tradition another mode of celebration came into vogue (we are not sure just when this happened)—the one specified in two texts: Genesis 17:12 and Leviticus 12:3. These state that *each individual father* (rather than the fathers as a group) is to enact this ritual with his own sons, and to do so, not at puberty, but when his son is still a newborn infant, on the eighth day of his life. In Israel, in other words, circumcision was transformed into an infancy ritual—it was something a father did for his own male children when they were still infants.

Can we assume that in this form it had a meaning similar or identical with that which it had (and has) as a puberty ritual? The association of this infant circumcision ceremony in Genesis 17 with God's promise to Abraham to give him a great progeny would suggest as much. Among the

Israelites too, in other words, procreativity and circumcision were intimately linked. This connection is also drawn in contemporary Jewish circumcision liturgies whose origins can be traced back into the first centuries of this era. According to Shoshana Matzner-Bekerman,[9] these begin with the mother bringing the child to the place where the ritual is to be performed. The child is then taken from her arms by an honored male guest, carried to another room where other male guests are assembled, and delivered to the father for the circumcision ritual proper.

At this point certain words are spoken that make quite explicit what its meaning is for the adults gathered. For example, at the opening of the ceremony the father prays, "Blessed be Thou, O Lord our God, King of the Universe, who has sanctified us by Thy commandments, and hast bidden us to make him enter into the covenant of Abraham our father." Those assembled reply: "As he has been entered into the covenant, so may he be introduced to the study of the Torah, to the marriage canopy, and to good deeds."

This particular prayer is repeated twice again during the remaining ceremony. Especially striking and surprising is the reference here to the "marriage canopy." In and through the circumcision ceremony the father declares his readiness to care for and nurture this infant son to the end that he will study Torah, eventually marry, and do good deeds. Thus, even though an *infancy* ritual, circumcision is performed with reference to that moment in life when this child will be a young adult, leave home and marry. It may thus be characterized as a puberty rite performed upon infants.

In other words, the biblical father does not wait until his son is an adolescent to prepare him for the decisive transition into adulthood, marriage, and a family of his own. He pledges himself to be involved to this end almost from the day of his son's birth. Circumcision is the mark of this paternal covenant between father and son.

## Passover

There was a third family ritual introduced into the Israelite family system early on, one which, in some respects, would eventually have an even more significant impact on the Israelite father-involved family than either of those we have discussed to this point—and that was the Passover celebration. Whereas redemption of the first-born was a ritual of the father carried out once in a lifetime (and only in connection with the eldest male child), and whereas circumcision was also a once-in-a-lifetime ritual for the specific male involved, the Passover ceremonies recurred annually and culminated in a festive family meal in which the entire family (wives, sons, daughters, and family servants) participated. These facts alone begin to suggest some of the reasons why this particular ritual has played the tremendously significant role it has in Jewish family formation and survival right down to the present.

What is stressed in the liturgical instructions for the performance of this ritual in Exodus 12 and 13 are certain actions by the fathers of the community prior to the meal itself. First, four days before Passover evening, a sheep or goat one year old is to be selected from the flock— one that is male and without blemish. Then, during the afternoon immediately prior to the Passover, the community of male fathers is to gather and collectively kill the animals they have selected, and roast them. In addition to this, blood from the slain animals is to be taken and smeared on the doorposts and lintel of each of the houses where the Passover lamb is going to be eaten. That same evening, after sundown, household by household, the roasted animals are to be eaten with unleavened bread and bitter herbs, within the confines and safety of the individual homes.

The texts describing this ritual go on to ascribe two meanings to this set of ritual actions, meanings that were to imprint themselves on the minds and hearts of its participants: (1) first of all, and in general, this meal was to be carried out as an act of remembrance of the time when God liberated his people Israel from Egypt; (2) but the meal was also meant to recall a quite specific feature of that liberation: those events related to the death of the Egyptian first-born and the sparing of the Israelite first-born. The texts recall that on the night of liberation a "destroyer" (as it is referred to in Exodus 12:23) ravaged the Egyptian households, killing all of their first-born sons, but this "destroyer" passed over the Israelites. In Exodus 12:21–28 this "destroyer" is pictured as a destructive force that would kill anyone who, on this particular night, left his house and went outside. Hence the urgent command: "Let none of you venture out of the house until morning" (Ex 12:22). The blood of the slain Passover lamb smeared by the father on the lintel of his house was regarded as a sign given by God as protection against this lethal danger.

It has been conjectured that Passover was initially an ancient rite of shepherds, enacted just prior to their going with their flocks to summer pasturage as protection against the nameless demons that might assail them as they traveled. If so, among the Israelites this rite was appropriated as a ritual of the family under the leadership of the father in memory of Israel's origins as a people through Yahweh's saving them from destruction during their escape from Egypt. Just as Yahweh acted for salvation, so does the father. He too must save his family from the destructive forces that threaten it. While Yahweh is the ultimate redeemer, the fathers must act too (if their families are not to perish) by gathering their families around them within the intimacy of the four walls of their respective houses.

No other ritual drama portrays as forcefully as does this one the interplay between God as father and the Israelite father in the care of his children. It is the culmination and embodiment of the other two rituals. If redemption of the first-born and circumcision are adoption rituals initiating the father into his role as custodian and guide of his sons in particular, Passover consolidates and expands that role, year after year, and makes it visible and accessible to the whole family, sons and daughters alike.[10] Through it fathers in Israel, as in no other culture we know of, appropriated to themselves an identity as redemptive caretakers, with an ongoing and permanent stake in the life of their families.

## The Teaching Father

From this there emerged in Israel yet another role for fathers of great importance for the future of Israel and the faith it represented: that of the teaching father. This is the second development in fathering I want to discuss briefly. A good approach to this subject, I have found, is to look first at what is known about educational practices elsewhere in the ancient world of this period. This can provide us with a backdrop for identifying what is similar or distinctive about developments within biblical culture.

A valuable resource for such a study is William Barclay's beautifully written book entitled *Train Up a Child: Educational Ideals in the Ancient World.*[11] From reading what he has written there, one is impressed, first of all, at how diverse were the educational ideals and practices of the peoples of this period and region (first millennium B.C.E.). Each culture, it seems, and in some instances different regions within a culture, had differing ideas regarding how children should be taught, what they should be taught, and who should teach them.

In ancient Sparta, for example, the focus of education was on preparing children to participate in or support a *military* elite. Everything was geared to that end. Those unfit for this goal were identified at infancy and killed. Even the fit, however, were not permitted to remain with their mothers, but were given to the care of nurses especially skilled in diet and discipline. At about seven years of age children would begin attending state-run schools for training in the martial arts exclusively.

In Athens on the other hand a very different set of goals and methods was operative. There the raising up of a male *cultural* elite was the goal; slaves did all the mundane jobs of the society. Free-born males were thus free to devote virtually their entire lives to music, aesthetics, philosophy, athletics and the like. Women, for the most part were excluded from these activities and confined to their homes and to caring for young children. Ideally, as the Greeks viewed it, the home was to be the first schoolroom, but in point of fact the family life of the ancient Greeks was so unstable, and women so ignorant, that little education took place there. Private schools for boys (from six to eighteen), where reading, writing, simple arithmetic, poetry, music and graduated physical exercises were taught, were the bastion of Greek education.

Roman educational ideals and methods were somewhat different from either of these examples. At least initially (prior to the third century B.C.E.) ethical and social values were stressed and the expectation was that a Roman father would be much involved in the education of his own children. Indeed, some of the more inspiring passages quoted by Barclay from Roman sources are portraits of fathers who tried to hold on to this older educational ideal at a point when it was dying out. An example is Plutarch's description of a certain first century Roman senator named Cato, who once declared that:

A man who struck his wife or his child was laying hands on the most holy of sacred things; that it was a greater honour to be a good husband than a distinguished senator, and that nothing was more admirable in old Socrates than that he lived in peace and quiet with a difficult wife and half-witted children. When Cato's son was born [Plutarch continued] no duty (save perhaps some public function) was so pressing as to prevent him from being present when his wife bathed the child and wrapped it in its swaddling clothes....As soon as the boy was able to learn, Cato took him personally in charge and taught him his letters, even though he owned an accomplished slave who gave lessons to many boys. But Cato, to use his own words, would not have the slave abuse his son, nor perhaps pull his ears for being slow at lessons; nor would he have his boy owe a slave so precious a gift as learning. So he made himself the boy's school master, just as he taught him the laws of Rome and bodily exercises; not merely to throw the javelin, to fight in armour or to ride, but also to use his fists in boxing, to bear heat and cold, and to swim against the current and eddies of a river. And he tells us himself that he wrote books of history with his own hand and in large characters, so his son might be able even at home to become acquainted with his country's past.[12]

However, in Rome as in Greece this noble educational ideal proved to be a difficult one to implement due to the influx of slaves, the disintegration of family life and the demands of the expanding Roman empire in the third and second centuries B.C.E. More and more, from that time onward, parents began hiring tutors for their children, or sending them to schools modeled on the Greek schools. Roman elementary schools, however, tended to focus almost exclusively on reading, writing and arithmetic, and the teachers were poorly supported by small fees supplied by the parents. These schools were also poorly equipped and extremely boring, writes Jerome Carcopino, since they met almost every day of the year (except for summer holidays) from dawn to noon, and there was an excess of time to master what little subject matter there was. As a result, he adds, most children carried away "the gloomy recollection of years wasted in senseless, stumbling repetitions punctuated by savage punishments."[13]

Looking at the educational ideals and methods reflected in various texts of the Old Testament in this light, what comparisons and contrasts might one draw so far as educational *goals* are concerned? It seems evident, to begin with, that education for *military* preparedness was not nearly as prominent in biblical culture as it was in Sparta, or even Athens or Rome. In fact, we read nothing in Hebrew scripture about fathers training their sons in the arts of war, or sword handling, or horse riding, or javelin throwing. Also, the cultural goals of Athenian education do not seem to correspond to what we find in Hebrew writings. While parents in Israel might well have taught their children to read and write, it is nowhere said that they did so, nor that they taught them how to play musical instruments or the like.

Rather, the educational goals of the biblical people seem to be closest to those of *ancient* Roman civilization. Proverbs 4 declares, for example, that what the grandfather told the father, and the father the son, was to cherish wisdom, by which was meant primarily knowledge of good and evil and how to avoid the path of evil and choose the good path which, it is said, "is like the light of dawn, its brightness growing to fullness of day" (4:18). This text also states that "more than all else" students should keep watch over their hearts "since here are the wellsprings of life" (4:23).

What may have been meant by such admonitions, more concretely, is outlined in Psalm 78:3–8 in sentences that read as though they were crafted as a kind of educational manifesto:

What we have heard and know,
what our ancestors have told us
we shall not conceal from their descendants,
but will tell to a generation still to come:

the praises of Yahweh, his power,
the wonderful deeds he has done.
He instituted a witness in Jacob,
he established a law in Israel,

he commanded our ancestors
to hand it down to their descendants,
that a generation still to come might know it,
children yet to be born.

They should be sure to tell their own children,
and should put their trust in God,
never forgetting God's great deeds,
always keeping his commands,
and not, like their ancestors,
be a stubborn and rebellious generation,
a generation weak of purpose,
their spirit fickle towards God.

Here then, perhaps, is a kind of overview of educational goals in Israel: first, to learn the basics about Yahweh, both what he represents in himself (his "praises" or titles), and what he did by way of past deeds and miracles, as well as what he gave to Israel by way of laws (hence, theology, history, morals)—and all this with the end in view that the children might come to trust in Yahweh and keep his commandments, and in turn pass this knowledge on to the next generation (hence also education, pedagogy).

I suggested above that this idea and approach would appear to be closest to the educational goals of the ancient Romans, but even in that regard one senses some significant differences. Israelite education was, it seems, much more concerned than was Roman education with cultivating in children, as a first priority, a certain attitude or feeling for *God*, for Yahweh. Hence a religious dimension played a much greater role in education here than elsewhere, it appears.

Most striking of all, however, in comparing Israelite education with that which developed in Rome or Greece, is the degree to which in Israel the ideal of the home as a setting for educating children was realized. While in Israel too there might well have existed publicly funded academies or schools for an upper class elite, during certain periods (in Jerusalem, for example, from the Solomonic era onward), strange to say, such schools are never explicitly referred to in our sources, and what is emphasized instead (in the biblical texts available to us) is the responsibilities that fathers and mothers have for teaching their own children.

In appraising this remarkable fact, the emphasis placed upon *both* parents as the educators of their children should not be overlooked. In the typical Greek family, as just noted, men *only* received an education in the schools, and even in Rome only the father is portrayed as teacher of his sons. By contrast, in biblical tradition children were instructed to listen to the teaching of their fathers *and* their mothers (Prv 1:8; 23:22; 31:26). This too is the point of the commandment which heads the list of social teachings that make up the second part of the decalogue: honor your father *and* your mother (Ex 20:12; Lv 19:3; Dt 5:16). In Israel such respect for both parents was regarded as one of the most important of all biblical teachings, next in rank to the command to honor God himself (see Lv 19:2f).

That fathers *and* mothers were so highly regarded as teachers in Israel implies that the family domicile was being thought of as a classroom of sorts. There where parents shared life on a daily basis with their children was the single most important setting for the education of children into what it meant to be an Israelite. This ideal is put forth with special clarity and passion in the biblical book of Deuteronomy. Of course, it is not the family residence *only* that Deuteronomy focuses on as the bearer of tradition. Communal festivals where laws are recited and covenants made are also identified in this book as having an important part to play in the education of this people (see, for example, Dt 27–28 and 31:9–13). But Deuteronomy seems to imply that it is in the family that education at its best occurs—and this because of the way in that setting instruction can occur at almost any time, while "at rest in your house or walking abroad, at your lying down or at your rising" (Dt 6:7), informally and personally in response to spontaneous questions (see Ex 12:26; 13:14). Here too, in the setting of the home, one is free to experiment in such matters as memorization by means of wall mottos, or the like (Dt 6:9f.; 11:18–21).

From this it can be seen why respect for *both* parents was regarded as so important in Israelite culture. This particular educational model requires a home in which a father and mother are present and both are completely familiar and at ease with the religious heritage, so that they can share it in an informal, relaxed and friendly manner in the course of daily life. Needless to say, it was the cultivation of strong, stable, father-involved families that made this educational model possible.[14]

## Concluding Comments

This chapter was begun with the suggestion that new modes of fathering began emerging in Israel in the wake of its experience of God as redemptive father. Through the rituals of redemption of the first-born, circumcision and Passover, fathers in Israel came to be involved with their families and children to a degree unparalleled in other cultures. In the course of time they also became teachers in their families, again to a degree that was unique. It might be said, in fact, that it was this emerging sense of responsibility for teaching among the Israelite fathers that gave rise to the Hebrew Bible itself. Thus the frequently noted pedagogical power of Hebrew scripture itself bears potent witness to a new and more vigorous involvement of fathers as caretakers of children in the culture in which this scripture was born.[15]

Eventually public schools *were* established in Judaism too, as elsewhere in the ancient world—at that point, in fact, when the Hebrew Bible had emerged and had begun to assume a paramount role of its own in Jewish life as sacred scripture. What happened to fathering, then, is the story I will be tracing in the next essay.

# 7.

# NEW MODES OF HUMAN FATHERING (NEW TESTAMENT SCRIPTURES)

*While highly supportive of the biological father-involved family, New Testament Christianity was more focused, it seems, on fostering the growth and development of vital spiritual families under the leadership of spiritual fathers and God as father.*

A glance at the book of Acts where the origins of Christianity are chronicled will indicate that Christianity began as a sect of Judaism, and only gradually emerged as a religion in its own right. In other words, the immediate background of the New Testament was not the Old Testament, but Judaism as it was beginning to develop in first-century Palestine. This being so, before turning to an analysis of what New Testament scripture has to say on the topic of fathering (the subject of this essay), it may be useful to note what was happening to father roles generally in the Judaism of this period.

## First Century Judaism

An important point to remember is that the Hebrew scriptures (Old Testament) were now a firmly entrenched religious authority, especially the Torah (first five books of Moses). All first-century Jewish sects

71

regarded the laws and traditions enshrined there as divinely revealed truth that required zealous study and application in daily life.[1] As a consequence schools and traditions of interpretation had already sprung up that would eventually rival in authority the scriptures themselves. It was in this way that there emerged those compendia of rabbinic insights and teachings, the Mishnah and Talmud, which were eventually to become as sacred to the Jews as were New Testament writings to Christians. While the final editions of Mishnah and Talmud were not completed until long after the books of the New Testament were written, it seems likely that many of the traditions referred to there were in place among at least some Jewish groups already during the period when Christianity was being born.[2]

What then do we learn from these documents regarding the way the role of the father might have been developing within certain sectors of the Judaism of this period? Fortunately, we do not need to guess at the answer to these questions, for there is a section of the Talmud devoted explicitly to this issue. In the Talmudic tractate *Kiddushin*, beginning with section 29a, there is a passage on the duties of father, where it is indicated that the rabbis of old had devoted much thought to such matters and had arrived at a consensus which specified that, with respect to a son, a father has five responsibilities: first, to circumcise him; then to redeem him (if the eldest son); third, to teach him Torah; fourth, to teach him a trade; finally, to find him a wife. Some rabbis added that a father should also teach his son to swim!

After stating these duties in outline form, the *Kiddushin* tractate goes on to discuss each one in greater detail. Special attention is devoted to the importance of the father's role as teacher of Torah and a trade. Both are regarded as essential to the son's future well-being. The duties of a father toward his daughter are also briefly touched upon. She too will need the father's attention and help, especially in finding a husband. "Let her be dowered, clothed and adorned," we read, "that men should eagerly desire her" (*Kiddushin* 30b). The detail and specificity of the document are impressive.

From this document alone it is evident that the father-involved family continued to occupy a central place in Jewish life. It was the primary locus of ritual action and instruction—"...a continuous, theocentric educational institution," as one scholar has described it.[3] Indeed, even though this was the era when synagogue schools were also begun, these did not replace the role of the father or the family as the primary setting of social-ization and learning, but were seen rather as supplementary. This empha-sis on the nuclear family and its role in spiritual formation has remained a unique feature of Jewish life and tradition right down to the present.[4]

# Christianity

It was in a social environment such as this that Christianity was born. In fact, it is not unlikely that it was in such a home headed by just such a Jewish father (as described in *Kiddushin* 29a) that "Jesus son of Joseph, of Nazareth" (Jn 1:45), founder of Christianity, lived and grew to matu-rity. Such was the case, at least, with that other great figure in the emer-gence of Christianity, Paul (or Saul) of Tarsus, apostle to the Gentiles (see what he says on this score in 2 Corinthians 11:22). Did then this emphasis on the father-involved family remain a trait of Christianity?

That it did not to the same degree is already hinted at by the fact that there is no single text in New Testament scripture quite like the Talmudic tractate we have just looked at. In fact, the paucity of New Testament texts that speak explicitly to or about fathers regarding their duties as fathers *of their own children* is a little surprising. This in itself may be significant, as I will suggest later on. Nevertheless there are New Testament passages that bear *indirectly* on this subject and I would suggest we look at these first of all.[5]

# The Gospels

Among passages in the gospels that bear *indirectly* on the role of fathers are the following:

(1) It is well known how Jesus spoke out against easy divorce and remarriage. "So then, what God has united, human beings must not divide" (Mk 10:9). Few religious leaders made this point more strongly.[6] In doing so he was also supporting, indirectly, the ideal of lifelong

monogamy and the father-involved family, for only as sexual unions are exclusive and enduring can men even begin to know who their children are, much less be significantly involved in their care.

(2) Jesus' words about the importance of children are also indirectly supportive of fathering in that they are spoken to his male disciples regarding *their* attitudes toward children. Indeed, Mark reports that Jesus was angry at his disciples for their distorted values in this regard. When they rebuked certain parents for bringing their children to him for his blessing (10:14), he told them instead: "Let the little children come to me; do not stop them; for it is to such as these that the kingdom of God belongs" (Mk 10:14). It was then that he also said that "anyone who does not welcome the kingdom of God like a little child will never enter it." Following this saying, we are told, he took the children into his arms and blessed them. This act of taking the children into his arms was a prophetic sign dramatizing just how important such children were to him.

A similar point was made on another occasion when these same disciples had been arguing over who would be greatest (Mk 9:34). True greatness, Jesus told them, consists of a servant-like attitude (9:35). "He then took a little child whom he set among them and embraced, and he said to them, 'Anyone who welcomes a little child such as this in my name welcomes me; and anyone who welcomes me, welcomes not me but the one who sent me'" (Mk 9:36f.) "To receive [or welcome] somebody" always means "hospitality, be it as a temporary guest or through adoption as a permanent member of the family," writes Hans-Ruedi Weber. "Whether he [Jesus] spoke of children in general or referred especially to children of the poor and to orphans is not specified," he adds, but "such hospitality for children and adoption were common practice in the Jewish environment of Jesus."[7] Clear, in any case, is the way this passage equates a receptive attitude toward children with a receptive attitude toward God. By implication, neglect or rejection of children is tantamount to a rejection of God. It is hard to imagine how the importance of caring for children could be stated any more forcefully (two Matthean sayings, Matthew 18:6 and 19, make the same point with similar intensity). A caring attitude by males toward children is an absolutely essential trait of the disciple of Jesus.

And yet it must be acknowledged that even here Jesus does not address fathers explicitly as to their role and duties as biological fathers of their *own* children.

(3) Still another way in which Jesus may be said to have spoken *indirectly* to the issue of fathering is through his own conduct as a man during his public mission. His whole demeanor was that of a certain kind of father. This shines through virtually everything he said and did: his healings, his approach to women, many of his best known stories and sayings. For example, the gospels occasionally preserve phrases in Aramaic (his mother tongue) that were uniquely memorable. One such was his word to a little girl whose parents thought her dead: *"Talitha kum!* which means, 'Little girl, I tell you to get up' " (Mk 5:41). Why was this tender word preserved in its Aramaic original? Perhaps because it was so characteristic of him. A core memory of Jesus was this authoritative, father-like, yet extremely tender way of speaking and acting. He was a certain kind of father—perhaps the father that many of the alienated of his time had not had and were inwardly secretly longing for.

Jesus likened himself to a physician. "It is not the healthy who need the doctor, but the sick..." (Mk 2:17). In another saying he alludes to himself as a shepherd on a mission to "the lost sheep of the house of Israel" (Mt 10:6). The sick he was trying to heal and the lost sheep he was trying to find were those of his contemporaries who were suffering because they could not cope with some of the new and stricter forms of Judaism then coming into vogue. From the point of view of this new religious elite the people attracted to Jesus were "sinners" and they had to wonder if Jesus himself was not one too (Mk 2:15–17). As a result a controversy developed, one that eventually led to his rejection and death.

But again, through this whole very difficult experience, Jesus remained remarkably firm, even tough and courageous at points, but always with a certain tenderness and grace that was highly touching and memorable, even life-transforming for some who experienced it for the first time. One might say that Jesus himself was a new kind of father—obviously moral and upright, certainly strong, even aggressive, but at the same time humble, compassionate toward sinners, and not as preoccupied with adherence to the details of Torah as were some of his Jewish contemporaries (Mk 7:14–23).

(4) The root of this new "fatherly" approach, Jesus himself declared in many different ways—and this too has a bearing on our theme—was a new understanding of the human predicament, on the one hand, and a new understanding of God, on the other. As to the human predicament, the whole issue of what defiles was a crucial one in Jesus' day (see Mk 7:1–23). Certain foods, contact with the dead, certain bodily emissions and the like were said in Hebrew scriptures to defile and make unclean. As well, certain cleansing rituals were prescribed for dealing with these defilements. Issues of this kind had become very important to certain sects in the Judaism of his time.

But somehow—and it is another of the little miracles associated with his career—Jesus managed to break free of this type of thinking without rejecting Torah altogether. His point of view seems to have been that it is not what goes into a man that defiles, but what comes out of him, out of the heart (Mk 7:14–16). Simultaneously he grasped afresh, perhaps through his own experience at his baptism, that by turning sincerely and humbly to God, even apart from obedience to every last law, God *can* be found and change of heart and forgiveness can be experienced (Lk 18:9–14).[8]

The God whom he himself found in this way was tenderly referred to by him not as Master of the universe, or Lord (the traditional way of addressing God in his time), but as Abba, the endearing word a small child used in those times in speaking to his father (or respected adults).[9] This Abba was the God of Israel, the God of Hebrew scriptures, but now experienced in a fresh, intimate, fatherly way. How Jesus felt about this God is movingly expressed in numerous sayings and parables, and especially, of course, in that most moving parable of all, his story of a prodigal son who was so generously received home by his father that his more upstanding elder brother was filled with consternation (Lk 15:11–32).

In this story especially, all that Jesus felt about both God as father and human fathering found a classic expression. It is something like this that he had in mind, no doubt, when he said to his male disciples, not: Be *holy*, as the Lord your God is holy (that was the motto of certain contemporary Jewish sects), but: "Be *compassionate* as your Father is compassionate" (Lk 6:36). Marcus Borg, in an important recent study, has referred to this as "the Mercy Code" and believes Jesus was quite deliberate in formulating it as a contrast to the Holiness Code.[10] In Jesus a new, more merciful type of father is revealed—or better, perhaps, revealed *again*, since God's gracious fatherliness is a prominent motif of the Hebrew scriptures as well.

(5) There is yet another piece of gospel data that must be mentioned as of some indirect relevance to this issue of fathering in the New Testament, and that is the fact that during the time of his public mission Jesus was both alienated, apparently, from his parental family (see Mk 3:19b–21), *and* unmarried—hence without an immediate biological family context. This unusual situation may have been due to a personal tragedy. It is quite likely that Jesus' father had died some years earlier, perhaps when he was still a teenager, before the time had come when his father would have arranged a marriage for him had he been alive.

As eldest son Jesus would have become head of his deceased father's family. It was possibly in that role that he grew to manhood and lived out his life during his later teens and twenties. This, I suggest, may be one of the reasons he never married, and also why when he left this role as his deceased father's surrogate to go out to John the Baptist, and then began his public mission, his mother and brothers and sisters were so surprised and perturbed (see Mk 3:19b–21, 31–35).[11]

Whether or not this hypothesis is correct, something like this must be in the background to explain the degree to which Jesus at this time of his life was in fact both alienated from his parental family and had no alternative biological family of his own. As he viewed it, in fact, the mission he was on, and the people who were gathering around him through his mission, were his *true* family, and were replacing his biological family (Mk 3:31–35).

Thus, already during the mission of Jesus there began to surface that rather sharp bifurcation between the biological family and the spiritual family that has remained a feature of the Christian movement ever since. It is apparent that for Jesus the spiritual family came first, the biological family second, so that if a tension should arise between them, there is no question as to what choice one must make. To a would-be disciple who wanted to bury his father before following him, Jesus said, "Follow me, and leave the dead to bury their dead" (Mt 8:22).

Here, I suggest, is a partial explanation for the lack of attention in the teaching of Jesus to the role of fathers as caretakers of their own children.

At the time of his mission Jesus was alienated from his family of origins and without wife or children of his own. He functioned instead as a spiritual "father" in the midst of a growing spiritual family.

In summary, while contributing powerfully to the strengthening of the father-involved family through his passionate sense of God's merciful fatherhood, his vigorous support of marital fidelity and his prophetic words about the importance of children, by failing to speak explicitly to the issue of a father's duties in his own family, and by drawing a contrast between the biological family and the spiritual family, the Jesus of the gospels could be interpreted as downplaying the one against the other.[12] I will have more to say about all this at the conclusion of this essay (and in the concluding essay of this volume).

## The Remainder of the New Testament

What of the rest of the New Testament? Are these new emphases that we have observed in the life and teachings of Jesus also found there? Do any new trends surface? The picture of fathering in the rest of the New Testament is remarkably consistent with the one just outlined, with a few supplemental touches here and there. The following are a few of the more important points reiterated.

(1) To begin with, Jesus' unique emphasis on the importance of enduring sexual bonds in marriage is clearly and forcefully represented there as well. In fact, in one of his rare references to Jesus' teachings it is to his sayings about divorce and remarriage that Paul appeals, in seeking to encourage marital fidelity among his Corinthian converts (1 Cor 7:1–11). Paul adds to this, in other passages, pastoral-type counsel for wives and husbands in the building of their relationship to one another and to their children. Wives should be prepared to defer to their husbands in certain respects, and husbands are encouraged to exercise a Christ-like leadership in the sacrificial way they love and care for their wives (Eph 5:21–33). Whatever one might think of Paul's advice in this sensitive area, he is obviously only intent on one thing: to see that his converts preserve a very high ideal of family life, one where husbands and wives are faithful to

each other and function harmoniously and lovingly together in their care of each other and their children (see also Col 3:18–21).[13]

(2) Also, needless to say, what Jesus said about *God* as father and about the graciousness of God, and about finding forgiveness and salvation through faith in this gracious God, is represented elsewhere in the New Testament on almost every page. In fact, one of the foremost features of these scriptures is just this amazing force with which this new understanding of God manifests itself.[14] "Father" has here become God's name, as in the Lord's Prayer: "Our Father, hallowed be thy name...." Indeed, even in the far-off Christian congregations of Rome the Aramaic usage of Abba which had been Jesus' own unique way of invoking God became a distinguishing mark of the Christian movement and a concrete sign that one had become a believer and a Christian (see Rom 8:15; Gal 4:6). Elsewhere Paul regularly refers to this same deity as "the Father of our Lord Jesus Christ." The mighty paean of praise to this God and Father in Ephesians 3:14–21 is just one of many examples of how New Testament scriptures exalt this aspect of the divine revelation that broke into history through Jesus. At the center of New Testament scripture is "the Father from whom every paternity whether spiritual or natural takes its name" (Eph 3:15).

(3) We look in vain, however, in these same scriptures (other than the gospels) for something comparable to Jesus' prophetic words regarding the importance of children.[15] In compensation for this lack, so to speak, we do have there something that is missing in the gospels: a few sayings, at least, addressed specifically to fathers as fathers regarding the fathering of their own children. Brief as they are, it is impressive to note that these say exactly what (from the indirect evidence we have garnered so far) we might expect to be said on this subject by people who had become followers of Jesus.

The first and shortest of these sayings in Colossians 3:21 is simply a warning to fathers: "Parents [fathers], do not irritate your children, or they will lose heart." The second, in Ephesians 6:4, repeats this warning, but adds a positive admonition: "And parents [fathers], never drive your children to resentment but bring them up with correction and advice inspired by the Lord." Apart from two passing comments in passages devoted mainly to other matters,[16] these are the only statements in the

entire New Testament spoken explicitly and directly to fathers as to their
responsibilities as caretakers of their own children!

It is not insignificant, perhaps, that what is identified in the first of
these sayings as a chief problem in fathering is a certain over-severity or
capriciousness that might be discouraging to children or arouse their
anger. "Fathers, take care that you not be overly severe." One recognizes
in this a continuation of that struggle against the unregulated power of
fathers *(patria potestas)* that was begun (within the communities shaped
by biblical faith) in the time of Abraham.

In the second of the two sayings devoted to this subject Christian fathers
are admonished to play an active role in raising and educating their children. The substance of their pedagogy is defined as "correction and advice
inspired by the Lord." The phrase "of the Lord" may allude to an instructional tradition originating in Jesus—perhaps the passing on of the kind
of stories and sayings that were eventually written down and assembled
in our gospels. Unfortunately this is nowhere stated in so many words, nor
is any further indication given as to what more precisely an education
informed by "the Lord" might entail. Either what was involved was so
well understood that nothing more needed to be said about it, or the
Christian pedagogical traditions were still vague and in flux. I might note
here, however, that it was vagueness on such issues that predominated as
a feature of the Christian movement for the next four centuries,[17] and there
remains a certain amount of confusion at this point among Christians
right down to the present. I will have more to say on this matter below.

(4) Another indirect way in which the new mode of fathering emergent
through Jesus was preserved and perpetuated in the rest of the New
Testament was through the teaching regarding the conduct and demeanor
required of men as spiritual leaders of congregations. It was through such
leaders especially that the model of fathering exhibited by Jesus himself
was chiefly perpetuated in early Christianity.

While passing reference is made to the qualities such leaders should
have as fathers in their own families (as for example in 1 Timothy 3:1–3
where it is said that they should be "husband of one wife" and able to
elicit obedience from their own children), the focus in this teaching is on
their generally good character and role as spiritual leaders. 1 Timothy
3:2–7, for example, specifies that men who have spiritual "oversight"

should be "temperate, discreet and courteous, hospitable and a good teacher, not a heavy drinker, nor hot-tempered, but gentle and peaceable, not avaricious, a man who manages his own household well." A comparable list is cited in Titus 1:7–8: never arrogant, or hot-tempered, nor a heavy drinker or violent, nor out to make money, but a man who is hospitable and a friend of all that is good, sensible, moral, devout and self-controlled. One might assume that such are the qualities as well that are now also being valued for men generally, and for fathers in particular, although this is nowhere said in so many words.

(5) In other words, here too (in the remainder of the New Testament outside the gospels) a certain tension persists between the home and the church, between the biological family and the spiritual family. This tension is strongest in the teachings of Paul, who like Jesus appears to have been without a family of his own during the time of his missionary endeavors, and who, in his earlier writings at least, advocated celibacy as an option for those who were able and suited to it (1 Cor 7:25–40). Certainly Paul does not disparage marriage and family, but it is nevertheless clearly intimated by him that tensions can and do exist between the necessities of family life and the requirements of a devout spiritual existence and that Paul preferred to see these tensions resolved in favor of celibacy and a life devoted to "pleasing the Lord" (1 Cor 7:32–35). So in this respect too the trends and emphases emergent in the gospels are perpetuated in the communities of the early church.

(6) There is one point, however, at which Christian thought in the period after Jesus went even further than he did in spiritualizing father-roles, and that is in the Paul-led movement to make circumcision optional as a family ritual among Gentile converts. The circumcision issue is so far behind us today, and biological father-rituals so foreign to our experience, that we forget that Paul's proposals in this regard were for a time the number-one issue confronting the early church. It is also often forgotten that in retrospect the decision reached at the famous Council of Jerusalem described in Acts 15 to go along with Paul in this matter opened up an almost irreparable breach between Jews and Christians (initially, in fact, between Jewish and Gentile Christians). Most Christians to this day appear to have little understanding of why this ritual was of such great importance

within Hebrew scriptural tradition, or why their Jewish brothers and sisters cling to it as tenaciously as they do right down to the present.[18]

## Summary and Conclusions

In summarizing what we have been trying to convey in this essay, it might be said that in Judaism and Christianity two new forms of religious tradition emerged, each springing from and strongly oriented toward the traditions enshrined in Hebrew scripture, yet with somewhat modified modes of fathering. In the one, Judaism, the biblical tradition of fathering was much more closely adhered to and even elaborated. For one thing the father-family rituals were strictly observed (circumcision, Passover and redemption of the first-born), and the father-role as teacher of Torah to his children was strongly endorsed and supported. Other tasks essential to the father-role were also delineated (teaching the son a trade, helping his children find spouses, teaching his son to swim).

In Christianity, on the other hand, the ties with Hebrew scripture were looser, although still intact. The visage of the father became more kindly and gracious. At the same time the family was diminished somewhat as the focus or center of religious life through the dropping away of fatherhood rituals and the shift of priorities to the spiritual family (congregation). The importance of the marital bond continued to be stressed, even more so, perhaps, with the instruction against divorce and the counsel for husbands to love their wives in a Christ-like manner, but with less emphasis on what specifically a father's role should consist of in relation to his own children. The importance of a receptive attitude toward children generally was powerfully emphasized in a few isolated teachings of Jesus, but only two pieces of advice, concretely, are to be found in the entire New Testament directed to fathers in their role as fathers of their own children. These caution them against being overly severe with their children, lest they become angry, and counsel that they be brought up in the discipline and instruction of the Lord. In this tradition more emphasis was placed on the qualities of men as spiritual fathers (or leaders of congregations or churches than on their role as biological fathers in their own families.

In trying to explain this shift of focus I have noted the fact that both Jesus and Paul, the principal figures in the emergence of the Christian tradition in the first century, although themselves products of strong Jewish families, were unmarried and without biological families of their own, it seems, at least at the time of their public missions. Their family was thus the community of those who were joining the family of God in the missionary movement of the church.

How shall we assess these developments? I believe they pose important questions for modern North American Christians as they try to cope with one of the most severe family crises since the dawn of the father-involved family. Undoubtedly, Christianity's focus on the spiritual family contributed significantly to its missionary success worldwide. At the same time, deemphasizing the biological family as it sometimes has may make it vulnerable to anti-family pressures in the cultures to which it has spread. This seems to be happening today. I will be commenting further on this subject in my concluding essay.

# PART FOUR
# CONTEMPORARY ISSUES

---

*Psychological fathering...is what the world is in need of more than ever in its history. There is a considerable body of scholarly evidence that civilization will stand or fall with whether such fathering is available in sufficient quantity.\**

*Edward V. Stein, "Fathering: Fact or Fable?" in *Fathering: Fact or Fable?* Edward Stein, ed. (Nashville, Abingdon, 1977), p. 11.

# 8

# THE CONTEMPORARY FATHERING CRISIS: THE BIBLE AND RESEARCH PSYCHOLOGY

*Fraught with difficulties in every generation, fathering today has become especially problematic, due to the impact on father-roles of the modern industrial and sexual revolutions. Yet, modern research psychology, in conjunction with the insights and support of biblical tradition, may be on the verge of releasing a new paradigm of fathering that will enable us to resist and even surmount these trends.*

My purpose in this essay is to attempt to indicate how three forces in North American culture—the Bible, research psychology, and a fathering crisis—are beginning to intersect in a way that could be highly important for our future well-being as families and as a society.

The Bible, of course, no matter how regarded, has been and still is an imposing "presence" in our civilization. As David Bakan has pointed out, it has "survived the test of the social equivalent of natural selection" by being "reaccepted more regularly and more reliably, generation after generation" than any comparable set of writings.[1]

By contrast, research psychology is an upstart. And yet, as a glance at the advice columns in our daily newspapers will confirm, it too is making its presence felt. For many it has already displaced the Bible as an authority in sexual and family relationships.

The contemporary fathering crisis, I hope to make clear, is only the most recent outbreak of father-deprivation, one of our oldest but still most portentous human problems. My thesis is that research psychology, responding in part to the contemporary fathering crisis, may be on the verge of releasing (in continuity with the Bible) a paradigm shift in our concept of fathering, a shift that could be of positive long-range significance.

But to understand why this may be so, we must begin our discussion, first of all, with several observations regarding the emergence in history of fathering.

## The Origins of Fathering

When did men begin functioning as fathers (psychologically as well as biologically) to their own children? The very question implies that a time existed when this was not the case. This clearly is so, and some awareness of this fact, and of the steps that may have led to fathering as we know it today, may afford us a horizon within which better to understand more recent developments.

Students of human culture point out that among the very oldest artifacts of antiquity a pregnant female figure is predominant (dating from the last ice age) and that the fecundity of women became an even more powerful cultural and religious symbol when agriculture was discovered.[2] For it was then that the fruitfulness of the soil was assimilated to the experience of women, and for millennia, Eliade writes, it was thought that Mother Earth gave birth by herself, through parthenogenesis.[3] It is only to be expected that during this cultural phase paternal representations are notable by their absence. A partial explanation seems to be that the role of the male in pregnancy is at this point still imperfectly understood, while the woman's role in the human life cycle is only too apparent.[4]

Hints of what family life may have been like under these circumstances can be derived from the observations of matrilineal tribes where the male's role in pregnancy is still unknown.[5] In these societies fathers are thought of as "guests" and the mother and her children (and her brothers) are the primary social unit.

But we can gain an even wider and sharper perspective by noting family patterns among certain highly developed primates, the African chimpanzees, for example ("our closest living relatives," according to anatomical, behavioral, and genetic affinities").[6] Here too a maternal figure is similarly predominant, for within the larger chimpanzee community of from thirty to eighty individuals it is the chimpanzee mother who is responsible for caring both for herself and the children born to her every three or four years (from the time she first becomes pregnant, at eleven or twelve, until she dies some thirty or forty years later). By contrast chimpanzee males spend their adult lives mostly moving about in small groups with other males, apart from the mothers and children, attending to their own needs. They pay little or no attention to their young. Indeed, they have no way of even knowing who their own offspring are, for when mating their contacts with females are brief, promiscuous, and socially inconsequential. It is the family unit of mothers and children that is clearly the chimpanzees' most enduring and important social unit.

The question persists therefore: If a family of this type (one in which mothers are dominant and males are marginal as husbands and fathers) was the historical starting point for the development of the human family, how and when did males begin fathering? One hypothesis is that a first step in this direction may have been taken *within* the kin group of mothers and children.[7] Andrienne Zihlman has proposed that, as early hominids began spreading out over wider territories in search of food, care of the young by the mother alone must have become increasingly difficult. If the maternal group was to remain intact and survive, older male siblings of necessity would have had to help. Selection, she suggests, would have favored those groups where this happened.[8] Since chimpanzee females determine to some extent with whom they mate and are frightened by the rather ferocious approach of some males, another factor in the advent of fathering, Zihlman adds, may have been female preference in sexual coupling for "those males who were more social and less aggressive and were [already] contributing to the welfare of their own kin group."[9] Although Zihlman does not say so, this would suggest that as child-caring males were selected as mates, they simply transferred their instinct for fathering from the maternal kin group to their own offspring.

However, the transition to fatherhood as we think of it today can hardly have been this simple. That additional complexities were involved is clearly intimated by those myths that everywhere in antiquity began to displace the earlier maternal myths referred to above. These are stories of heroes, all men, who typically do some great deed, such as slaying a dragon, for which they are rewarded with a female (or females) to mate with from their own age group.[10] *These indicate that as a condition for fathering a certain development had to take place in masculine self-consciousness.* The dragon (or its equivalent) in these myths, Erich Neumann proposes, is symbolic first of all of the mother, and that it had to be killed betrays the degree to which her hold on the psychic life of male children in particular (under the conditions of an increasingly prolonged childhood) had become problematic. Before men could begin fathering, a masculine style and identity *apart* from their mothers had to be fashioned, and this occurred, Neumann argues, within the autonomous male groups, led by older males (fathers of sorts), under the conditions of foraging, hunting and fighting that were unique to them.[11]

Just how important this step was to the development of fatherhood is indicated by the fact that it was during this same period of antiquity that puberty rituals which have played such an enduring role in the human family were fashioned. Their purpose too, we now realize, was quite simply to facilitate the transition of males out of the maternal group to the world of men, and then to families of their own.[12] In addition, the growing awareness (perhaps as animals were domesticated) of the function of the male in reproduction, as well as the phasing out of the female fertility cycle (making possible an increase in sexual relating) must have also played a role (as frequently noted) in men becoming more intimately and consistently involved with their wives and children. Ancient traditions and laws protective of the rights of those involved in this new social unit of mother, father and children bear eloquent testimony as well to the simultaneous emergence of the community or state and its role in this revolutionary development.[13]

However, right on down to the present, in the human family, emotional ties of sons to their mothers continue to be so powerful and the autonomy achieved so tenuous that relations to their "second families" (that is, to their own wives and children) are frequently fraught with problems. This is the condition that confronts us almost everywhere we turn when we examine more closely the inner dynamics of family life in the great majority of human societies, both ancient and modern. To one degree or another in ancient Mesopotamia, Canaan, Egypt, and Greece,[14] in modern Africa, India, China, and Japan (to mention but a few examples),[15] fathering remains among humans an often precarious, tension-filled role, while females regularly perpetuate the intense maternal traditions that are exemplified among the chimpanzees. Only through insights arrived at in this century are we now in a position to say, more precisely, why this is so.

But before turning to that, I want to look briefly at the place of the Bible in this unfolding history of fathering.

## The Bible and the Origins of Fathering

Most people today are aware of the fact that the Bible is the literature of a people (Israel) living in close contact with the wider culture of the ancient Near East during an axial age spanning roughly two thousand years (the second and first millennia B.C.E.).[16] So far as fathering is concerned, generally speaking, the matrifocal family is by now a thing of the past. Men typically, in these cultures, marry and are husbands of one wife and fathers to their own children.[17]

But it does not follow, as often imagined, that fathers were thereby firmly established or secure as ruling patriarchs in these families. On the contrary, the prevailing stories and myths of the ancient Near East often characterize them as weak and ineffective in comparison with their more powerful sons, wives, and daughters.[18] Sons especially are singled out in many of these stories as particularly unsettled and ambitious. Gilgamesh, in the Gilgamesh Epic (a story widely circulated in the ancient Near East during the second millennium), is a case in point. He tyrannizes his city with his undisciplined energy before finally setting off with a peer on a long journey of adventure and discovery. Fathers in the story are depicted mostly as watching helplessly on the sidelines.[19] Also, while fathers are everywhere titularly in charge, their rebellious, adventurous sons, not they, are the ones *really* ruling in heaven and on earth (again according to the myths and legends).[20] In short, the ancient Near East taken as a whole gives the impression of still languishing in a cultural phase more determined by heroic, somewhat grandiose, militant sons than by confident, effectively caring fathers.[21]

But is this the best that can be hoped for in human family dynamics and culture?[22] It is in answer to this question, I suggest, that the Bible enters the picture. In its pages we read of an ancient Near Eastern people who broke free of the prevailing myths. And what enabled them to do so, they testify, were events and revelations (Ex 20:2) that persuaded them that the strongest, most benevolent power at work in the universe (and the *one* power therefore to be seriously attended to, Ex 20:3) is neither son, daughter, nor mother, but a unique *father*-God who is compassionately and effectively involved and concerned with the welfare of his children (Ex 34:6f; Dt 32:6; Jer 3:19; Is 63:16; Mal 2:10; Lk 11:2; Eph 3:14f).[23]

Through faith in this God the role of human fathering in the biblical community was gradually transformed. Males, first of all, became more secure (Prv 14:26), and hence less needful of heroics in establishing their identities. To walk humbly with their god, and, like him, to care for others became the male cultural ideal (Mi 6:8).[24] With greater self-confidence (grounded as it was in a source that transcended the family) there came also greater freedom among Israelite sons to "leave father and mother" and become "one" with their wives (Gn 2:24). As a consequence, marital fidelity and love were progressively extolled (Prv 4:18–20; Gn 2:24; Song 8:6f; Mal 2:13–16) and women generally were less feared and more appreciated by men as their "counterparts" or equals (Gn 2:18–23).[25] For this same reason sexual conduct disruptive of marriage (rape, incest, adultery, homosexuality, transvestitism, sodomy) was identified and opposed to a degree unprecedented in the ancient Near East.[26]

It is only to be expected that children born of such marriages, in the setting of this faith, would also be afforded a protection and care that was equally unique. This expectation can be verified, first of all, through the fact that infanticide, still widespread in ancient times, was abolished by the Israelites (Gn 22:11f; Mi 6:7; 2 Kgs 23:13).[27] But also in less tangible ways Israelite husbands began to complement the child-caretaking roles of their wives. From the beginning in Israel, it seems, fathers thought of themselves as spiritual guardians of their families and symbolized this through their priest-like roles in family rituals such as consecration of the first-born (Ex 13:1f, 11–16), circumcision (Gn 17:9–14), weaning (Gn 21:8), Passover (Ex 12:1–14), and unleavened bread (Ex 12:15–20; 13:3–10). Child discipline too was increasingly seen to be the father's rather than the mother's primary task, for, it was said, "the rod and reproof give wisdom but a child left [by a father] to himself brings shame to his mother" (Prv 29:15; cf. 23:13f).

But above all, fathers in Israel became teachers of their children, not primarily in that more sophisticated mode exhibited in the book of Proverbs but through daily contact and informal conversations between themselves and their children (Dt 11:19), prompted more often than not by questions posed by the children themselves (Ex 12:26; 13:14; Dt 6:6–9, 20f). The basic content and purpose of these conversations is movingly summarized in Psalm 78:4–7, where fathers declare that what they had heard from their fathers should be shared with the next generation: namely, the titles of Yahweh, his power, his mighty deeds, and the decrees and laws he has instituted in Israel, all of which, in the telling, they stress, awakens confidence in God and ensures that his achievements and commandments will never be forgotten.

God himself is characterized as just such a compassionate teaching father in Hosea's portrait of the way, when Israel was an infant, he chose him, fed him, embraced him, taught him to walk, and, as Israel grew older, instructed him "with leading strings of love" (Hos 11:1–4).

It was this paternal passion for teaching in Israel that in the course of time gave birth to a body of literature—the Bible—one which may be characterized, quite simply, as a body of writings produced, for the most part, by fathers for sons or younger fathers, with the purpose, broadly speaking, of instructing them in fathering (or caring).[28] Eventually, through Judaism and Christianity, these writings were disseminated worldwide, and wherever their influence spread, mother, son, and daughter deities faded as consciousness of the divine father grew. This in turn brought about the transformation in masculine attitudes and family values that had given birth to the Bible in the first place: the bonds between men and women in marriage were gradually strengthened, as were men in their roles as caretakers of children.[29]

## The Contemporary Fathering Crisis

During the last century, however, influences have arisen in most modern societies severely challenging these biblically inspired trends. Foremost among these are the industrial revolution and now, in its wake, a far-reaching sexual revolution.

The initial impact of the industrial revolution on family life was devastating, as whole families were herded into mills and factories. But even with the introduction of child labor laws and compulsory education during the nineteenth century, it has continued to make family life difficult in a number of ways. First, due to the necessity now of moving about in pursuit of work, the nuclear family (fathers, mothers, and children) was often dislodged from its extended family network of grandparents, uncles, aunts, and cousins. This weakened the ties between generations and diminished the involvement of older people with younger families.

At the same time the nuclear family itself was reshaped significantly because of the way the place of work was separated from the family residence. In many older societies families worked together, fathers and sons in one sphere, mothers and daughters in another, both in geographical proximity (as is still the case today in family farms and businesses). When during the later phases of the industrial revolution children were kept out of the labor force and sent to school and it became customary for mothers to stay home while men alone (for the most part) went off to work, this had the effect of isolating fathers from wives and children. Under these conditions women, until recently at least, tended to revert to their archaic role of primary caretakers of children while men gravitated to male groups and a sphere of life outside the home. A degree of father deprivation unknown in many pre-industrial societies was the result.[30]

Into this social milieu burst the sexual revolution in the late 1960s and 1970s. Their ties to family already strained by conditions brought about by the industrial revolution, and spurred on by the availability of birth control strategies of one kind or another, males (and females too, of course) began questioning the necessity of confining their sexual activity to one spouse only. In a single decade in North America (between 1971 and 1979) the ideal of sexual celibacy before marriage, until this point a pillar of the American family system, was abandoned as a prevailing cultural norm.[31]

Several consequences quickly followed: marriages became more fragile, divorce rates accelerated, and out-of-wedlock pregnancies increased dramatically.[32] This in turn resulted in an alarming increase in single-parent families, the vast majority of which were mother-led.[33] Another consequence is now also in sight: growing numbers of father-deprived children with overly intense and therefore more problematic maternal ties that endanger their emotional development (more about this later).

It is this combination of trends, I suggest, that constitutes our contemporary fathering crisis. While millions of children are deprived of appropriately caretaking fathers by conditions brought about by the industrial revolution, millions more are virtually being abandoned by fathers caught up in the sexual revolution.

## Research Psychology

It is well known that powerful reactions to this crisis are already in motion and have been for some time. Women themselves (in this century especially) have been fighting back, both by challenging the more devious pursuits of their male counterparts (alcohol, gambling, pornography) and by pressing for a more autonomous lifestyle and equal rights for themselves.[34] During the last decade (for this and other reasons) they have also been entering the workforce in unprecedented numbers, and this alone has been a critical factor in forcing men to reconsider their roles in family caretaking responsibilities.[35] Even independent of this, however, men themselves, perhaps, disillusioned by their experience in a depersonalized, technologized society, have in recent years been gravitating toward aspects of parental experience often denied them. An especially notable example of this is the growing number of men now sharing more intimately in the birth experience of their wives. It should be noted that in communities inspired by the Bible (church and synagogue), powerful movements have arisen in recent years challenging men as seldom before to pay more attention to their families.[36]

But another important voice, I suggest, is also being heard in the land, one that because of its base in the university and the deference in our culture to scientific authority, may be as important as any. This is the voice of research psychology where an awareness has been growing, in recent years, of the importance of fathering in human personality formation.

At the beginning of this century when research psychology was still it its infancy, Freud already discovered how essential fathers were to the formation of conscience in young children during their so-called oedipal years from three to six (more about this later). But research psychologists were slow to capitalize on these discoveries, partly because of their origins in seemingly (to some) abstruse therapeutic conversations, but also because the society generally was more focused on maternal roles in child-care than on fathering. Even as late as 1965 John Nash, a research psychologist who pioneered in the study of father-roles, could lament the lack of concern about fathering on the part of his peers and attribute this to little or no interest in the subject in the culture at large.[37] Since then, however, there has been a dramatic change. Psychological research on fathering has mushroomed during the last several decades, so much so that it has already generated a remarkable set of insights, some of which are beginning to inform the actions of increasing numbers of parents.[38]

Of these, broadly speaking, two stand out, I believe, as of very special importance for the future of fathering: the first having to do with *when* fathers should ideally become involved in parenting their children, the second with *how*.

As to when: Freud's breakthrough discovery (already referred to) of the father's role in conscience formation had already alerted researchers to the fact that paternal involvement in children's lives was essential quite early if they were to grow up able to "work and love," at least as early as the oedipal years from four to six. A wealth of recent studies not only confirms this judgment,[39] but suggests that fathering is important even earlier, indeed from birth onward. This research of course in no way diminishes the well-established fact that mothers too play an irreplaceable role in the lives of infants and young children. Their capacity for unique emotional closeness and sensitivity in caring (conveyed through countless acts of feeding, smiling, talking, caressing) are in fact decisive in establishing that bedrock of security and trust in children that is foundational for everything else.[40]

But what is clear now is that fathering too, during this very same period, has an equally important *complementary* contribution to make in at least three ways.

First, by simply being there as a significant "second other" for their infants to relate to, fathers can help them, even during their very first months, to put distance between themselves and their mothers and so make a solid beginning on the road to maternal separation and individuality.[41]

Second, fathers are virtually indispensable in helping their children control and come to terms with their still wildly fluctuating aggressive impulses, during their "terrible twos" especially, when internal ego-controls are still fragile.[42]

Third, through their special sensitivity and concern for gender distinctions fathers contribute immeasurably to the crucial formation of firm body-congruent gender-identities in both sons and daughters.[43] This, we now realize (and it is among the most important psychological discoveries of recent times), does not happen automatically. Gender itself, of course, is a biological given, but gender-identities are formed in response to subtle distinctions in parenting (many of them father-initiated) during the eighteenth to twenty-fourth months of children's lives, before, in most instances, children can even talk.[44]

Closely related is a sobering illustration of the importance of fathering for sons in this earliest age period (1–3), one afforded by the ongoing research into the origins of homosexuality in men. While still a matter of dispute, the search (since Freud) for the genesis of this orientation has repeatedly and consistently identified as one of its causative factors a pattern of parenting, early in life, characterized by weak or absent fathers and over-involved mothers.[45] Freud, however, focused on the way this parental pattern makes it difficult for boys to identity with their fathers during the so called oedipal years (3–6). More recent research has underscored the impact of such parenting on children even earlier. Socarides, for example, reports that two-thirds of the approximately four hundred adult homosexual men he has counseled suffered from a blurring of the boundaries between themselves and their mothers and acute gender confusion—and this is due, he writes, to an experience with "crushing mothers" and "abdicating fathers" already during the very earliest pre-oedipal years of their lives. "The father's libidinal and aggressive availability," he writes, "is a major requirement for the development of gender identity in his children, but for almost all pre-homosexual children the father is unavailable as a love object for the child."[46]

So urgent is a child's own felt need for a father during these first years that one researcher has termed it "father hunger"[47] and another likens the father in his role at this time of his children's lives to that of a lifeguard rescuing a child desperately trying to reach shore while being pursued by a dragon.[48] In this light it is not insignificant perhaps that the first word children say, typically, is not mama, but daddy (or its equivalent) and the first picture that absorbs them is again the father's, not the mother's.[49] When men abandon their families at this age and stage, it is not unusual for their children to have terrifying nightmares from which they awaken screaming for their fathers.[50]

But not only has research psychology, in recent years, underscored the importance of an *early* involvement of fathers with their children, it has also begun to generate a number of insights regarding the *kind* of fathering that is needed. This facet of the research is best illustrated, perhaps, by what is now seen to be required of fathers during the oedipal years from three to six. It is then, as Freud first pointed out, that children typically entertain romantic thoughts and emotions toward the parent of the opposite sex, while experiencing competition, even hatred, toward the same-sex parent. For children to have such emotions is an important step in self-discovery, for it is through this that they can begin to visualize their potential for becoming men and women with a procreative and parental destiny of their own. However, to realize that potential, children must also rather quickly begin to undergo an emotional transformation whereby they let go of the opposite-sex parent and become reconciled with the parent of the same sex, thereby internalizing the renunciation of incest and murder—the core of a healthy conscience. Both to affirm these ascendant oedipal emotions but then also to facilitate their transmutation are among the most complex and consequential challenges confronting the nuclear family.[51]

In the case of a boy, Freud thought, the lever that brought about these important changes (that is, the eventual detachment from the mother and rapprochement with the father) was fear of being castrated by the father should he (the son) persist in the maternal attachment. This indeed is a factor in some instances, but then, too, identification with the father will often turn out to be precariously ambivalent. This is the inner condition that typically presents itself in counseling with adult male neurotics, where affection for the father, if present at all, is often interlaced with resentment and a strong tie to the mother. A major development in recent research is the verification that this is by no means the only, nor even the optimal way that the resolution of the oedipal drama may proceed. Boys with firm but also friendly and supportive fathers have a much easier time identifying with them and letting go of their mothers than boys with fathers who are too stern and disciplinarian.[52]

Girls too during this oedipal period can derive a great deal of self-confidence from their fathers, if, once again, the fathers are not just strong, but warm and supportive. Girls, however, in contrast to boys, must eventually desexualize the paternal tie and let go of their competitive posture toward the mother if they are to recover an identity more in line with hers and marry someone in their age group.[53] This requires, on the father's part, in addition to his encouraging stance, a certain reserve, if he is not to inhibit her development at this crucial stage. Even so, as Lora Tessman points out, the "remnant attachments of her love for him are sometimes not completely swept away until the daughter herself is married and her rapprochement with her mother may need to await the time when she has given birth to a child and is secure in a maternal role of her own (this because of regressive fears that mothers can reactivate in both sons and daughters).[54]

Even these few comments should make it clear that fathering, especially from the oedipal years onward, is a complex and subtle task with important long-range consequences. As to the kind of fathering that is needed, at least four characteristics may be deduced from the above observations: to father well, fathers must be (1) involved, (2) assertive and strong (rather than passive), (3) affectionate, and (4) capable of fostering a loving bond between themselves and their wives.

That fathers should be involved with their children should be obvious but unfortunately is not—many in our culture seem oblivious to the importance of father roles in the healthy maturation of their children from their earliest years onward. Affectionate assertiveness and strength are required of fathers above all to foster autonomy and to counteract the tendency of mothers and children to hold on to each other.[55] Affection, as just noted, facilitates the paternal identifications and attachments of both boys and girls so necessary to their sexual identities and self-confidence. Finally, a father's bond with his wife insures the fulfillment of their own sexual-emotional needs in such a way that generational distinctions are firmly maintained and their children's efforts at having one or the other for themselves alone (the essence of the oedipal situation) are frustrated.[56] At the same time it provides a model for children of what they may look forward to when they are older and ready to get married themselves.

The father's role in the life of his children does not end with the oedipal years. During latency (seven to twelve) he continues to be needed as friend, mentor, and guide, and during early adolescence his loving firmness, if present, will again serve as a shield and support for the working through of the autonomy and role-identity issues that first surfaced in his children during their oedipal years.[57] Only as children marry and become parents themselves does the paternal role begin to shift significantly from that of caretaker to something more akin to facilitator. However, even then, with the advent of grandchildren, an "unambivalent admiration and love of young children" (as one researcher has put it) may be powerfully revived, energizing fathers (now grandfathers) to complement in significant ways the parenting provided by their own adult children.[58]

It is with these psychological benefits and realities in mind that Antoine Vergote, a leading religious psychologist, has aptly characterized the father as the primary agent in our progressive humanization.[59] And this too is why Edward Stein, another religious psychologist, has written that the presence of the right kind of fathers in sufficient numbers, during the coming years, may well determine whether our civilization will stand or fall.[60]

## A Paradigm Shift

At the beginning of this essay I wrote of a paradigm shift in our concept of fathering that may be coming to birth through the conjoint midwifery of the Bible and psychology. In this concluding section I will try to clarify more precisely in what sense this might be true.

The Bible, it was stated earlier, through its revelation of God as effectively caring father, may be viewed as fostering, within the broad sweep of history, a generally stronger, more confident, more faithful type husband and father. However, viewed in the light of what is currently known about fathering through research psychology, it can be seen that even the Bible is not as clear, at some points, as we now realize we must be if fathering is to be optimally effective. The two issues just discussed in the previous section are a case in point: *when* fathering is important, and *what kind* of fathering is important.

Concerning the "when" of fathering, it will be recalled that, like research psychology, the Bible also, in certain passages, emphasizes the importance of fathers becoming involved with their children *early* in their lives. However, nowhere does it specify *how* early, and this, as we have seen, is an issue of considerable consequence. It is tragically evident in the light of what is now known, that fathers in most cultures (whether biblically influenced or not) become meaningfully involved with their children *too* late. Already at five, for example, maternal over-investment, coupled with paternal deprivation, may have had such a disturbing effect on a child's emotional development that it will suffer from it for the rest of its life. In highlighting the importance of fathering for children during the very first years of their lives, research psychology has given precision and force to the biblical maxim that promises that if fathers take an interest in their children while they are still children and direct them in the way they should go, they will not depart from it even when they are old (Prv 22:6).

However, similarly unclarified in the Bible, in some respects, is the issue of what kind of fathering is needed. While rightly stressing *both* forcefulness *and* friendliness as paternal modes, it must be admitted that a certain ambivalence comes to expression in the biblical portrait of fathering, an ambivalence which has lent itself to a variety of interpretations and cultural expressions. More specifically: a certain pedagogical severity in fathering may be garnered from certain texts (Prv 22:15; Heb 12:7–11), while a more relaxed, compassionate fathering is gleaned from others (Ps 103; Eph 6:4).[61]

The place of corporal punishment in childrearing may serve to illustrate the issues at stake. Several biblical passages advise a generous use of the rod without specifying more precisely how generous, at what age, or under what circumstances (Prv 22:15; 23:13; 29:15). How at least some fathers in Israel interpreted this counsel (and not the least learned ones either) can be seen in the redoubtable Jesus ben Sira's stern words on parenting. If a father truly loves his son, he writes, he should avoid playing with him or sharing his laughter, but rather be strict with him, correct his mistakes, bend his neck, bruise his ribs, and beat him frequently (Sir 30:1–13).

As noted, research psychology also emphasizes that fathers should be assertive and firm, but intimates as well that the kind of firmness that may be called for during the "terrible twos," for example, may not necessarily be appropriate at five, six or sixteen, and that children of any age, when punished too much, or where paternal friendliness is missing as a basic mode, may have difficulty relating to their fathers as positively as they should if they are to experience that bond with them that is so essential to their healthy self-esteem and development. Again, therefore, the insights of research psychology lend credibility to certain biblical emphases while also helping us appropriate them with greater finesse.[62]

Needless to say, as the women's movement of our time is reminding us, a third point at which the Bible is somewhat deficient has to do with its relative neglect of both mothering and the father's role in the life of daughters. It would be wrong, however, to interpret the biblical emphasis on father-son relations as necessarily prejudicial to women, in the light of what is now known of the importance of a secure self-identity in men as a precondition of their ability as adults to respect women generally and to marry and become caretaking fathers. But certainly a gap in our knowledge is being supplied by the increasingly vivid picture being painted in research psychology of the complementary roles of fathers and mothers in childrearing and, more particularly, the father's significant contribution to the emotional well-being of his daughters as well as his sons. As this is more widely understood, it may help ease the anxieties of those women who fear that biblical father-religion may somehow be detrimental to their own best interests. On the contrary, as we now know, good fathering facilitates good mothering and contributes to the humanization of both men and women.[63]

These are some of the ingredients I see in the paradigm shift in our concept of fathering alluded to earlier. *On foundations laid by the Bible, research psychology is helping us see not only that fathering is important but that it is important early in the life of children in modes that are firm but friendly—for daughters as well as sons.*

It might be noted in conclusion that if it is true, as the evidence suggests, that such fathering, when it is present, helps children grow up more confident, more capable of working selflessly and creatively, better able to marry and care for their own children, then this only confirms the biblical promise that those shall live long in the land who have available to them a father of this kind, along with a mother, to honor, and respect (Ex 20:12).

# 9.

# IN DEFENSE
# OF MONOTHEISTIC
# FATHER RELIGION

*Viewed in the light of its capacity to support and encourage
healthy personal growth to maturity for both men and women (as
this is illuminated by key insights from developmental psychoanalysis)—and considering the alternatives—faith in God as
caring gracious father appears to be an optimal form of religion
for both men and women.*

## The Problem

In biblical religion (and consequently western religion) worship rises to a
solitary, transcendent, benevolent father. This is true of Christianity no
less than Judaism. Although Christianity has sometimes been described as
a "son" religion, it is nevertheless that of a son who mediates to the father
(1 Tm 2:5).[1] Many questions, however, are now being raised about the
religious, social, and psychological effects of such an exclusive emphasis
on God as father. Women are increasingly concerned about the possible
detrimental impact of such a religion on their lives in particular. Would
their needs not be better met, they are asking, if this highly patriarchal
focus were modified, either by introduction of a corresponding matriarchal element, or by abandoning the patriarchal image altogether?[2]

In this brief essay I propose to examine this question from the point of
view of certain key insights from developmental psychoanalysis.

Viewed in this light, I shall argue, monotheistic father-religion may be more supportive of the emotional well-being of women (as well as men) than it is sometimes portrayed to be.

## Psychoanalysis

The justification for a developmental psychoanalytic approach to this issue lies in the illumination that has come to us from that source concerning the respective roles of father and mother in the emotional maturation of children.[3] They are by no means the same for boys and girls, and therein lies a critical and often neglected element in the current debate.

For boys, a key phase in their progress to maturity, according to psychoanalysis, is the sometimes rather traumatic transfer of affection and trust from the mother to the father during the so-called oedipal years from three to six. Thus by the sixth year of life, the boy typically acquires a secure masculine identity, is liberated for a non-incestuous, guilt-free sexuality, and goes on eventually to become a husband and father in his own right.[4] The girl, too, at about the same time in life, also detaches herself from her mother by means of a trusting, loving relationship to the father. But for her this relationship marks not the end but only a passing phase in her journey to maturity. It is crucial to her emotional development that she move beyond the father, in a kind of oedipal loop back to an identity more in line with her mother. Were she to remain with the father, she, like the boy who is tied to his mother, would find herself caught up in an incestuous web that would inevitably inhibit her identity as a woman and her freedom for sexual love.[5]

These few observations already allow us to draw at least two conclusions regarding the way monotheistic father religion typically intersects with key phases in the emotional development of children:

1. Insofar as both boys and girls must put emotional distance between themselves and their mothers as a first step in reaching maturity, and insofar as the father in both cases plays a significant role in the "individualizing" process, invoking God as benevolent father may

be viewed as playing a constructive, supportive role in the psychological formation of both sexes.

2. However, insofar as women, in contrast to men, must at a certain point move beyond the father to complete their identity, the evocation of God as father, in their case, could have an inhibiting effect at this stage in their development.

This would suggest that patriarchal monotheism does indeed confront us with a dilemma. While it offers an emotional environment uniformly helpful to men in surmounting their most crucial and difficult developmental challenge (rapport with the father), it could have a retrogressive effect on women by threatening to anchor them still deeper in an oedipal tie to the father that must eventually be terminated if they are to come into their own. This, I suggest, is the crux of what needs to be dealt with in the current debate in western religion over the gender of God.

## Presuppositions

In considering this issue, however, attention must be paid first of all to certain basic presuppositions of the religious tradition we are talking about. These are, I suggest, that God is personal and one and is to be worshiped as such by both men and women. *This means that so far as this religion is concerned any recommendation regarding the gender of God must be evaluated from the point of view of its overall capacity to mediate a meaningful unified personal reality to both sexes.* This obviously restricts the alternatives that might be considered. Excluded by these presuppositions, for example, would be the now frequently advocated androgynous option, for there is simply no solid basis in human experience for relating to a *personal* reality that is both male and female, or neither, or fluctuates between the two.[6] If God is "person" and that person is one, only two figures have an analogous "ultimacy" in actual human experience to that of God, mother and father.[7] And while these personages overlap, they are not the same: at crucial points in the emotional journey of children (during the oedipal years especially) they are required to play distinct, complementary roles. To fulfill their respective tasks in the human life cycle fathers must be fathers and mothers must be mothers. *Thus, a choice must be made, in a personal monotheistic faith, between father or mother as the ultimate symbolic configuration.* The only question is which it shall be. Are there psychodynamic factors that would favor one over the other as the preferred religious environment for *both* sexes? I think there are.

# Defense

To begin with, because of the chronological and experiential primacy of the mother in the birth and initial care of children, a son's emotional bond with his mother is typically more intense than a daughter's tie (during the oedipal years) with her father. As a consequence, it is emotionally more traumatic for a son to achieve a secure sense of male identity and become oedipally liberated than for a daughter. Father-religion is, therefore, of more critical importance as an emotional support system for men than mother-religion is for women. At the same time, and for the same reasons, mother-religion is more threatening to masculine identity than father-religion is for the identity of women.[8]

However, it would be quite wrong if this observation were to leave the impression that women should forego mother religion and more or less endure father religion for the sake of men. Actually, mother-religion is not an altogether favorable emotional environment for women either.[9] While it is true, as noted above, that women need to break free from their fathers and find an identity more in line with that of their mothers, this can happen in a meaningful way, as already noted, only *after* they have been freed from an overly dependent maternal bond through a good relation with the father. And then, women do not typically reidentify with the mother in an emotional, wholehearted way (as, say, the son does with the father) because of the threat of a renewed loss of independence. The role of the mother in helping her daughter find her identity is therefore an important but, at the same time, a restricted one. Other factors are of equal or even greater importance.

I refer in particular to the roles that men play in feminine identity formation, a subject often overlooked in feminist discussion of this topic.[10] The point I now want to make is this (in summary): not only must men face a more difficult challenge than women in resolving their own oedipus complex, but it is of paramount importance that they do so because of the key roles they must play (as both fathers and husbands) in helping women resolve theirs. I have already called attention to the rather complex process by which women typically form and then terminate their bond with the father and then move on to become women and mothers in their own right. I have also noted that this requires, in the first place, a father who can (during the oedipal years) relate to his daughter in affirming but non-incestuous, non-binding ways. I have not emphasized, however, how important it is, if a father is to play this role appropriately, that he has himself worked through his own oedipal emotions and established an uninhibited sexual relation with his wife. Otherwise the danger is great that he will foster a relationship with his daughter that is characterized by the same incestuous dependencies that tie him to his mother.[11]

Even with the best of fathering, however, the daughter's bond with her father has a tendency to linger—in part this is because of the already mentioned threat to her independence that is involved in any renewed identification with her mother.[12] More often than not, therefore, her tie to the father is terminated (and her status as a woman in her own right confirmed) only when she is "courted" and married and becomes a mother herself.[13] But this, too, requires men who are oedipally liberated, for those whose maternal bond is still strong and whose identification with the father is tenuous invariably turn out to be either insecure and anxious, and as a result frightened of women, or tyrants desperately intent upon proving themselves. *Nothing is more devastating for the emotional well-being of women than such men. While this psychic condition is what some writers seem to have in mind when they castigate western father religion, this is in fact the situation that prevails where the role of the father is tenuous and threatened by matriarchy.*[14]

Authentically secure fathers, rather, foster oedipally liberated males capable of courting and loving women in a manner that frees them from parents for an enduring marital relation of truly autonomous persons. Furthermore, a mature husband in a vital bond with his wife, far from prolonging the emotional tie with his daughter, will actively foster her freedom. In providing, as it does, an emotionally supportive milieu for the attainment of these utterly essential goals, monotheistic father religion,

I suggest, may be viewed as an optimal form of religion not only for men, but for women as well.

## Implications

It is beyond the scope of this brief essay to spell out the implications of these observations for the actual functioning of men and women in a community devoted to a benevolent father deity. But in concluding it might be noted that in the light of the above at least some of the practices of both Judaism and Christianity may not be as onerous as they are sometimes portrayed. That, for example, in both communities women have traditionally not been at the emotional focal points of worship and leadership is not necessarily to be interpreted as implying an inferior status on their part. Rather, with the previously mentioned psychoanalytic observations in mind, this could be seen as the expression of a healthy sensitivity to the fact that it is, generally speaking, in everybody's best interest, in a father religion, for the women to be more detached and objective in their spirituality.[15] It is the men who must be challenged to lift up "holy hands" in prayer (1Tm 2:8), not only for their own good but for the sake of the women whose emotional freedom is so vitally dependent on theirs.

# 10

# THE REFUTATION OF THE "FATHER" IN GOD IN FEMINIST THEOLOGIES AT THE END OF THE TWENTIETH CENTURY: ANALYSIS AND CRITIQUE

*Certain fault lines in feminist theologies (misconstruction of what fathers are; neglect of developmental issues and needs in the lives of children; flawed analysis of the origins of patriarchy) suggest why refuting the "Father" in God has proven easier than filling the religious and social void left by his absence.*

## Analysis

The expression, "the refutation of the 'father' in God," in the title of this essay is taken from a monologue of the nineteenth century European philosopher Friedrich Nietzsche in *Beyond Good and Evil,* where he poses the question, "Why Atheism Today?" and states by way of an answer what he says he learned through a great many conversations, namely, that "The 'father' in God has been thoroughly refuted....Also his 'free will': he does not hear—and if he heard he still would not know how to help. Worst of all: he seems incapable of clear communication: is he unclear?" Nietzsche asks, and replies, "This is what I found to be causes for the decline of European theism...."¹ Nietzsche went on to suggest what he thought would be the consequences of this refutation—not the *end* of religion, but the emergence of new religions. "The religious instinct is indeed in process of growing powerfully," he wrote, "but the theistic satisfaction it refuses with deep suspicion."²

It was to fill this void that Nietzsche put forward his own passionately conceived "Philosophy of the Future," at the center of which stood his famous *Übermensch* (Superman), a powerful, self-willed type of man whom Nietzsche describes as utterly disdainful of pity and willing to enslave others for the sake of a truly civilized elite that "will grow, spread, seize, become predominant—not from any morality or immorality but because it is *living* and because life simply *is* will to power." In a defining moment in the middle of the twentieth century, when these ideals were embraced and put into effect by men of this type, the world experienced the alternative to the demise of the "father" in God that Nietzsche had been talking about and proposing.³

I begin this essay with these comments because it would seem that something analogous is happening as the twentieth century draws to a close. The "father" in God is again being "thoroughly refuted," this time, however, not because he is perceived to be too weak and does "not hear," but because he is thought to be too powerful, and that, as such, he privileges men and demeans women and legitimates the unjust sexism that permeates western culture. Thus, in the opening pages of her book, *Sexism and God-Talk, Toward a Feminist Theology*, Rosemary Ruether graphically portrays God as a domineering, blustering male seated on his cosmic throne and "bellowing" (her word): "I am the Lord thy God, Thou shalt have no other gods before Me." This, she says, is the monotheistic ogre who has presided over our androcentric culture for the past several millennia, and only when he is dethroned will women be able to realize their full humanity and equality with men and the world will become what it is meant to be.⁴ A similar warning is sounded in the writings of feminist theologian Elisabeth Schüssler Fiorenza. "A Christian symbolic universe that proclaims an Almighty, Father-King-God whose will and command is revealed in the texts of scripture," she writes, "religiously legitimates and reinforces not only misogyny, but also racism, status inferiority, homophobia, and xenophobia."⁵ She calls upon

Christians to reject this universe of "kyriarchal" language and structures.

However, in this instance refuting the "father" in God has proven
easier, it seems, than filling the void left by his absence.[6] "We are about
to learn what happens when father-gods die for an entire culture,"
states Naomi Goldenberg in her book, *Changing the Gods, Feminism
and the End of Traditional Religions*,[7] but what she goes on to observe is
taking place is a "turn toward inwardness" from which a multiplicity of
variously gendered (or genderless) gods or god images are emerging,
none of them predominant as yet, and some less benign than others.[8]
"Image-making itself," she concludes, may be the only common
ground achievable among the devotees of these varied religious alternatives.[9] Ruether writes similarly of a "plurality of identities" and of
the need for a "praxis of multireligious solidarity and syncreticism."[10]
Schüssler Fiorenza calls for "a discourse embodying a variegated
'reflective mythology.'"[11] The collapse of "normative assertions" within feminist theologies is increasingly evident.[12]

Only slightly less inchoate are the alternative social visions being
espoused in these theologies. *Human* fathers (like the father in God)
are viewed as *males* whose power is excessive by virtue of "legal,
social, economic, and political relations that validate and enforce the
sovereignty of male heads of families over dependent persons in the
household."[13] Hence fatherhood is thought of as unjustly legitimated
male power over others which must be dismantled for women to realize their full humanity and equality with men. What women now want,
writes Ruether, is to "tear down the walls that separate the self and
society into 'male' and 'female' spheres."[14] To do this, "demands not
just a new integrated self but a new integrated social order" in which
males and females play virtually interchangeable roles, and "maleness
and femaleness" will be no more than "reproductive role specialization"
with "no necessary...psychological or social role differentiation...."[15] In
a similar vein Schüssler Fiorenza calls upon Christian theology to
"rearticulate" its symbols, images and titles for God and Christ in a way
that "deconstructs the Western cultural sex/gender system."[16]

Analogous psychological and societal ideals are expressed by gender
philosopher Sandra Lipsitz Bem, whose book on this subject envisions a

"gender neutral" society in which the distinctions between male and female are so "completely dismantled that—except in narrowly biological contexts like reproduction—the distinction between male and female no longer organizes either the culture or the psyche."[17] Bem recognizes, of course, that "biological contexts like reproduction" do pose problems, for, "Only women can experience pregnancy, and its impact on a woman's physical condition is such that if not taken into account institutionally, it automatically advantages men as a group and disadvantages women as a group."[18] The care of infants and children poses similar "institutional" problems, she notes. The solution advocated is professional child care paid at a much higher rate than is now typically the case, along with compensatory advantages for the women needing to sacrifice themselves in this manner (as she puts it).[19] In this emergent vision, family strength is not judged "by its traditional form (whether there are two parents)," writes Janet Giele, director of the Family and Children's Policy Center, Brandeis University, "but by its functioning (whether it promotes human satisfaction and development) and whether both women and men are able to be family caregivers as well as productive workers."[20]

Recent theorizing on this subject brings to mind Plato's thought-experiments in *The Republic*, written some 2,500 years ago.[21] For him too the societal ideal was full equality of women and men in all spheres of human culture (education, athletics, commerce, politics, war)—and he too realized that for this to happen radical new ways would have to be found for dealing with the incapacities resulting from women's role in pregnancy, childbirth and care of young children. He was also of the opinion that the two-parent father-involved family was expendable and that alternative ways of having and caring for children might be devised that would allow women to be less tied to the domestic role of mother. The problem could be solved, he imagined, by the state supervising certain days of sacred assembly when those duly certified for reproduction would gather for this purpose. Fathers would no longer know or care about who their children were, and the women impregnated by these sexual encounters, in order to return to their roles with men in the larger society, would divest themselves of their maternal responsibilities as quickly as possible by transferring their infants to state orphanages run by professionals.

## Critique

That Plato could imagine that gender equality might be achieved in this manner says a great deal about his insensitivities to aspects of the human social and emotional condition: the bonds between husbands and wives; the affections of parents for their children; the ways in which gender functions to anchor personal and emotional identities and children benefit from the affections of both parents and suffer without them. There are reasons why Plato's equalitarian vision has never been implemented. In our time too the feminist crusade against the "father" is bound to abate or be modified as the fatherhood crisis deepens and it becomes ever more apparent how indispensable fathers are for the psychological and social well-being of their children.[22] In the meantime, however, the crusade will continue and its attacks will inevitably center (as they have thus far) on that literature which feminist scholar Phyllis Bird states still "marks the line of most aggressive resistance to feminist goals," namely, the Bible.[23]

Feminist theologies may be divided into two groups, states theologian Ted Peters. The first openly rejects the biblically based religious traditions of the West, believing as they do that the full liberation of women will require an entirely new religious gestalt such as worship of the goddess, or a bi-gender or genderless divine symbol system; the second, while holding similar views, affirms the basic tenets of biblical faith, but "in doing so seek[s] to keep, but weaken the divine father symbolization."[24] It is this second, more insidious refutation that will be the focus of the following critique.[25] I will be discussing three "fault-lines" in feminist theologies of this type: (1) the misconstruction of what fathers actually are and signify; (2) the neglect of developmental issues and needs in the lives of children; (3) and third, a flawed analysis of the origins of patriarchy.

## The Misconstruction of
## What Fathers Actually Are and Signify

Peters notes two steps in the strategy of those feminist scholars who "seek to keep, but weaken the divine father symbolization" in the scriptures and liturgies of western, biblical religion; "both [are] taken at the level of critical consciousness," he writes.[26] Step number one is "to put distance between the symbol and its referent, between language about God and the being of God...." What is stressed is that God's own being is "ineffable, infinite, indefinable, mysterious, not subject to univocal statements." It follows that God "is not literally 'our Father.' The term *Father* is just a metaphor or symbol." The second step follows closely, he states. It involves the manipulation and interchanging of symbols and metaphors for God. In the process the Father image is demoted and non-patriarchal images are advanced. "It is, in short," Peters summarizes, "a divide-and-conquer method."[27]

The ineffability of God is not to be challenged or questioned. All language for God (all language, in fact) is analogical, drawn from human experience and no more than an approximation of the reality to which it points. On this there is no disagreement.[28] But this does not mean that all God-language, all metaphors, all analogical approximations are equally adequate, meaningful or true. *When speaking to or about God, some analogies are more appropriate, more adequate, more meaningful, more conducive to evoking or "naming" what God really is than others.* And whether consciously or not, we do make judgments in this regard, both as individuals and collectively, so that over time specific ways of naming and talking about God inevitably take hold and become distinguishing features of given cultures or civilizations. The Bible is a case in point. Its pages reflect a culture in which distinctive ways of invoking, addressing and thinking about God were embraced and then advocated, after a prolonged struggle with religious alternatives similar to those being advanced today.[29]

The God central to these scriptures is *named.* Yahweh (the name), used some six thousand times in the Hebrew scriptures, is not Baal (connoting son), not Ashteroth (connoting mother), not Anath (connoting daughter). Yahweh is El (connoting father). The identification of Yahweh with El the god of the fathers (Ex 3:15) and the father of the gods (Gn 33:20; Jos 22:22) is very explicit in the biblical narratives. The assumption that the ascription of fatherhood to God, admittedly pervasive in the Greek New Testament scriptures, is infrequent in the Hebrew scriptures is the result of an oversight in this regard. The name Yahweh itself connotes "father." When asking, "Have we not all one

father, has not one God created us?"(RSV) the prophet Malachi was
simply stating the obvious (2:10). The presumed answer is, "Yes, of
course; we all have one Father, one God created us."[30] It was thus most
natural for Jesus as well to teach his disciples to pray, "Our Father, hallowed be thy name" (Mt 6:9), and for Paul to greet his Gentile converts
with, "Grace to you and peace from God our Father" (Rom 1:7; 1 Cor
1:3; 2 Cor 12; Eph 1:2; Phil 12; Col 1:2). The centrality of this name
throughout the corpus of biblical literature is the reason why pronominal
references to God are *always* masculine—not because God is male, but
because God is father (Yahweh).[31] It is "he" (the father) who is rock-like,
warrior-like, husband-like, mother-like. It is "he" (the father) who
revealed himself in and through Jesus Christ as a friend of sinners. Father
is his name. It is simultaneously a function. God *is* a father and acts *like*
a father.[32] "As tenderly as a father treats his children, so Yahweh treats
those who fear him" (Ps 103:13).

The centrality of this name accords with the "intuition" (or revelation)
that invoking *this* gracious God bearing *this* name and following in his
ways is life-enhancing for individuals and cultures. The biblical stric-
tures against worshiping "other gods" bearing other names, connoting
other roles and espousing other values is not simply that they are alien,
but that they are inadequate, deviant, potentially destructive (Dt
30:15–20), "empty cisterns that hold no water" (Jer 2:13). Adhering to
Yahweh alone will bring "blessings," not "curses" (Dt 28). "Look, today
I am offering you life…" (Dt 30:15). *The assumptions underlying this
biblical naming of God are thus just the opposite of those calling for the
refutation of the father in God. The late twentieth century characterization of this "name" as symbolic of male power demeaning for women
and destructive of their well-being is one that is in direct conflict with the
biblical assumption that this way of naming and thinking about God is
life-enhancing—and not just for men, but for a whole society.*

Whose assumptions are correct? These can be empirically tested by
looking at communities in which each of these assumptions is operative. Destroy the "father" in God and in culture and see what happens.[33]
See what happens in societies where God is honored as caring, gracious father and human fatherhood is vital and strong. The assumptions
can also be tested by careful analysis. We can think through what

fatherhood is and represents. This ought to be the focus of an intense debate, but feminist literature to date is notable for its neglect of this issue. The term "father" itself is avoided in feminist theologies. Instead, as noted, we read of androcentric families led by *male* heads of families whose dominance must be curtailed.[34] To be sure, the man who becomes a father *is* a male, but a male of a certain age and stage.

It is thus already a distortion and manipulation of the symbol father to define it solely as male. A father is a male who is such not just by virtue of his maleness, nor even by virtue of his insemination of a female. A father is such by virtue of the recognition accorded him as progenitor of certain children by a certain woman and who is himself receptive to this identity. For this to happen *knowledge* of the male role in insemination is required. The very concept "father" does not even exist without this knowledge. But even with this knowledge fatherhood can occur only when a specific woman admits a specific man into the reproductive process and accords him a recognized status as father of *her* children. Fatherhood is thus not even possible apart from the willing deference and collaboration of a woman with a man.

Fatherhood occurs at the conjunction of two relationships, writes anthropologist Peter Wilson in *Man, the Promising Primate*, the sexual pair-bond between a man and woman and that of the primary bond between a woman and her child.[35] It is the overlap of these two relationships that produces the *possibility* of a third—that between father and child. "This third relationship differs from the other two in that it is mediate, the product of the conjunction of the other two, which are immediately generated by the biological conditions of reproduction, nurture and attraction." Pair-bonds (between adult males and females) and primary bonds (between mothers and children) are rooted in nature, whereas the bond between a father and *his own child* is a socio-cultural event arising solely from a male's pair-bond with the child's mother.

Wilson's remarkable conclusion is that the identity and relation of father and child were thus the elementary *social* relationship in the evolutionary emergence of human beings from their primate ancestors, a relationship constructed by transforming natural circumstances and 'materials' through thoughts and promises. It is for this reason that he identifies human beings in their uniqueness over against all other orders of life as "the promising primate." It is this socializing capacity, he argues, which distinguishes human culture from primate existence.[36] In summary, fatherhood arises as a potential new mode of social relating (a male's recognition and care for his own progeny) from promises made between specific males and specific females with respect to their children. Used of God, the term "father" evokes an analogous sense of God's covenantal care and love for all he created. He is "the Father, from whom every fatherhood, in heaven and on earth, takes its name" (Eph 3:14f).

## The Neglect of Developmental Issues and Needs in the Lives of Children

I have been speaking of the misconstruction of what fathers are and signify in feminist writings. I want now to address what I regard as a second fault-line in feminist theologies: the neglect of developmental issues and needs in the lives of children. A recently published dictionary of feminist theologies (the first of its kind), with articles on virtually every facet of feminist thought, has not a single article on children or the developmental needs of children. Nor is there an essay on "father" (or the father's role in the care and maturation of children) to complement its essays on "mothers/motherhood," "mothers at home," "mothers in the workplace." In these essays it is assumed that women are the preeminent parent and can function well in that role with or without the fathers. "Furthermore," we read, "because God calls each woman to tasks that fit her gifts, there are a variety of ways to fulfill one's vocation as mother: adoption provides an equally valid alternative for becoming a mother to that of giving birth; lesbians are as capable of becoming good mothers as heterosexuals; single mothers can provide a loving home as well as married mothers...."[37] These sweeping assertions are presumed true without corroborating evidence or argument or attention to the actual needs of children. Instead, these essays are preoccupied with issues related to women's freedom to be or not be mothers. Their focus is on *adult* women achieving personal fulfillment through autonomous equalitarian relationships. "Feminism celebrates woman's ability to conceive, bear, and nurture children without making it a requirement for achieving true 'womanhood.'"[38]

This preoccupation with the equalitarian needs of adult women and the corresponding neglect of the developmental needs of children in feminist theologies is puzzling. Women are acutely conscious of the fact that during pregnancy, birth and infancy children are utterly dependent on them. Are they not equally aware of the enormous imbalances that exist at this stage of life as well, between mothers, fathers and their children, male and female alike? No relationship on earth is more symbiotically intense than that binding children to their mothers. Seen in this light the problem of imbalances of power between the genders takes on a wholly new aspect. How do children (male children especially) become autonomous human beings with appropriate gender identities and emotional strength to live fulfilled, happy lives on their own, as adults, apart from their mothers? How can fathers enter helpfully into this unique, symbiotic relationship? Failure to attend to these issues has been and still is a most troublesome feature not just of feminist theologies but of American culture generally, as Hans Sebold (among others) has noted in his book, *Momism: The Silent Disease of America.*[39] While children obviously need mothers for acquiring not just life but that bedrock of security and trust that is foundational for living,[40] just as obviously wives need husbands and children need fathers for acquiring strong inner identities and a sense of autonomy.

Fathers facilitate the human journey to maturity in many ways, among them: (a) first, by simply being there as companions to their children's mother and, right from the start, as "significant other" in the whole important process of infant socialization;[41] (b) second, through fostering secure body-congruent gender-identities in that critical eighteen-to-twenty-fourth month of children's lives when this must happen if it is to happen at all. Gender itself, of course, is a biological given, but gender-identities are formed in response to subtle distinctions in parenting (many of them father-initiated) right when children are learning to talk.[42] (c) A third way in which fathers facilitate the journey to maturity is by their limit-setting (in ways mothers cannot and still be there as unconditional caretaker) especially during the "terrible twos" when ego-controls are still fragile and not yet internalized;[43] (d) and fourthly, by fostering through their bonds with their wives (and in close harmony with their wives) those relationships with their children (during the crucial oedipal years from three to six) that will enable these children to begin to let go of their transitional romantic attachments to the parent of the opposite sex and become reconciled with the parent of the same sex, so that they are then free to move on into a future in which *their* potential for a procreative and parental identity of their own can be realized. There are by now a wealth of studies confirming the reality and importance of these momentous transformations during which the core features of conscience (the inner restraints against violence and adultery) are born.[44] It is difficult enough for these transformations to occur in children's lives in homes where caring fathers are present—the difficulties are greatly intensified by their absence or abuse.[45]

## Flawed Analysis of the Origins of Patriarchy

In addition to the misconstruction in feminist theologies of what fathers are and what their importance is for the healthy maturation of children, there is a third fault line in these theologies I want to try to say something about, even though in this instance the complexities are daunting. I refer to the analysis of the origins of patriarchy. Feminist scholars are currently locked in an unfinished and seemingly unresolvable debate over the history of the patriarchy which they describe as "rule of the father" *(pater)* and which they decry. Recognizing as they do that all known civilizations are characterized by the presence of families "headed" by such domineering fathers and believing as they do that the power-imbalances this entails must be rectified, they wonder how it happened that men became so dominant over women in the first place and why the problems in this regard are so entrenched—and what society was like before this happened. The quest for answers is obviously of great importance, for it might offer the key for dismantling the patriarchal edifice that now exists.

The assumption usually made is that there was indeed a time when men's and women's relationships were in fact more egalitarian than they now are, and hence various reasons are proposed for explaining what brought about male dominance. Religion scholar Rita Gross, for example, in her recent book, *Feminism and Religion,* focuses her search for an explanation on the emergence some five thousand years ago of newer labor intensive technologies—the plow, use of draft animals, complex irrigation systems, and the like—technologies, she writes, which favored men as the primary producers and increased the demand on women to bear children. In other words, as she sees it, patriarchy arose on the wings of changed "*material conditions* [which] promoted male dominance for the first time."[46] This suggests, she writes, that patriarchy is "the product of changing cultural and historical circumstances, rather than a timeless human condition...."[47] For her this means that through feminist thought and praxis, and under changed historical circumstances, egalitarian ways once pervasive in the human species are and can be recovered. However, missing from her analysis is any serious consideration of the term "father" (pater) as such, or of what was required for men to take on this role, or what does in fact transpire in a society when males do become fathers and the father-involved family emerges as a predominant, characteristic institution of a given human culture.

It is this latter set of considerations that is the focus of Gerda Lerner's erudite analysis of patriarchal origins in her book, *The Creation of Patriarchy*.[48] Lerner writes of her surprise that patriarchal origins did not lie (as she had thought) in acts of male assumption of power in the more usual sense, but, as she puts it, "in the appropriation by men of women's sexual and reproductive capacity." This, she writes, was prior to everything else and must be regarded as the key step in the rise of patriarchy. It is thus *her* conviction that for patriarchy to come to an end and for women to regain their full equality with men, an alternate form of social organization to that of a family in which women are sexually subservient to men will have to be found. Lerner is unsure what this will be and therefore less certain than is Rita Gross of what lies ahead. "What will come after, what kind of structure will be the foundation for alternate forms of social organization we cannot yet know," she writes on the final page of her book.[49]

Missing in both of these works and in feminist theorizing generally is an awareness of what ethicist Don Browning calls the "evolutionary ecology" of the two-parent family.[50] In other words, in tracing the history of patriarchal origins feminist theologians do not go back far enough to that point in time when males were completely absent from the family unit of mothers and played no role whatsoever in family life as we know it today. This, I suggest, is one of the reasons why in feminist accounts of patriarchal origins the problematic, as well as the uniqueness and irreplaceable nature of the two-parent father-involved family, is so vastly underestimated. Throughout the lower orders of life on earth males for the most part have no stake whatsoever in the care of their own offspring. This too is what we find among the higher primates, and even among the chimpanzees (our closest living primate relatives) where males roam in groups and mate randomly and are absolutely marginal to the life of females and their offspring.[51] This, it seems to me, is the starting point for any proper analysis of what we are contending with in what is now called patriarchy. Patriarchy, which can also be translated as "father origins" or "origins of the father," has to do with the long evolutionary development by which fatherhood was born and institutionalized as a distinguishing feature of the human species.

For this to happen, profound changes were required. For one thing a new kind of sexuality had to emerge (the phasing out of the estrus cycle), making possible more enduring male-female pair-bonds, before males could even begin to become part of the social group of women and children and fatherhood was even a distant possibility.[52] For example, evidence has been cited for suggesting that pair-bonding and family groups of this type (inclusive of males) existed as early as four million years ago,[53] but if the archaeological studies of Marija Gimbutas are to be trusted, men were still at the margins, and women were still at the core of community organization and child-care in Old Europe as recently as ten thousand years ago. The social structure was still matrilineal, Gimbutas writes, "with succession to leadership and inheritance within the female line."[54] The preeminent religious and cultural symbol was that of a pregnant mother with large breasts, who created life "out of herself."[55] More striking still is the fact that these conditions were still the prevailing ones among isolated tribes in the Trobriander islands of the South Pacific which anthropologist Bronislaw Malinowsky found and studied at the beginning of this century.[56] In these tribes, although men lived in sexual pair-bonds with women, promiscuity was rife, and the men were not thought of as the fathers of the children born to the women with whom they were living, since it was still believed that women bear children of themselves. In fact, Malinowsky reports, the word "father" did not even exist in the language of these tribes. Children regarded the male living with their mother as her "friend"—their lineage was traced through their mother's family only. This is as clear an example as I know of what human society must have been like prior to the institutionalization of the father-involved family as we have known it in western culture until recently.

Our oldest evidence of a decisive break and transition from such essentially fatherless, matrilineal forms of human society to those characterized by a family unit in which a male joins a female in a covenanted relationship oriented toward the care of children that are recognized as his as well as hers comes from those regions where the biological link between male insemination and the origins of a fetus were clearly understood and intentionally and culturally appropriated by the larger society through laws and traditions that were supportive of the father-involved family.[57] Evidence of what this entailed is apparent in the legal and wisdom literature of the peoples who settled the Egyptian and Mesopotamia river valleys some five thousand years ago.[58] Law codes and instructional texts from these regions dating to the third and second millennia B.C.E. (such as the eighteenth-century Mesopotamian *Code of Hammurabi* and the twenty-fifth century Egyptian *Instructions* of the *Vizier Ptahhotep*) bear witness to the enormous importance of the institutionalization of the father-involved family in the emergence of these first great civilizations.[59]

The father-involved families we encounter when reading the first books of the Bible were heir to these cultural and institutional innovations. Through Israel's encounter with Yahweh at Sinai and, subsequently, with the promiscuous cultures of Canaan, her own ideals in this regard (first consolidated through traditions and laws in the pre-Canaanite period) were shaken, then solidified and canonized (during Israel's second temple reforms), then channeled to future generations through the Bible's wealth of stories and teachings.[60] Especially with the advent of Jesus Christ and expansion of Christianity these ideals were shaped, intensified (in certain ways) and disseminated to Europe and America and then increasingly worldwide. Ernst Troeltsch in his history of The *Social Teaching of the Christian Churches* characterizes Christianity's contribution to father-family formation in European and western civilization as the modification "from within" of the "idea of male domination by its teaching about love and good will," so that "the patriarchalism of natural authority gives place to the patriarchalism of love, with its emphasis upon voluntary subordination and the duty of looking after the welfare of others." In the process, he writes, "the relationships themselves become softened and humanized."[61] It is this five-thousand-year history of the two-parent father-involved family that is now being tested and questioned as seldom before.

## Concluding Comments

At the beginning of his recent book of meditations, *Crossing the Threshold of Hope,* Pope John Paul II appeals to his readers not to be afraid to call upon God as father—and then, near his book's end, he writes again about this subject. Here he speaks of "original sin," which he characterizes as a most disruptive force in the life of humanity, because, he states, it wants to diminish or eradicate the "rays of fatherhood" that shine forth from God into the life of the world. Then (in italics), he adds, *"This is truly the key for interpreting reality,"* for "original sin is not only the violation of a positive command...but... *attempts...to abolish fatherhood,* destroying its rays which permeate the created world, placing in doubt the truth about God who is Love and leaving man only with a sense of the master-slave relationship."[62] My own thoughts in this essay may be viewed as an exposition of the truth of these insights. Like the state that protects us from anarchy, the father-involved family is a predominantly *cultural* (or spiritual) institution that protects us from dehumanization. It can be weakened or abolished, or it can be affirmed, embraced, nourished. Just as there are no more meaningful indices of a healthy culture than one in which fathers are present with mothers in the care of their own children and the institution of the two parent father-involved family is firmly established and strong, so there is no more meaningful name by which to invoke the God who lovingly leads us into our human future than as "father," "Our Father, who art in heaven, hallowed be thy name, thy kingdom come...."

# CONCLUSION

*The dreariness of the family's spiritual landscape passes belief. It is as monochrome and unrelated to those who pass through it as are the barren steppes frequented by nomads, who take their mere subsistence and move on. The delicate fabric of the civilization into which the successive generations are woven has unraveled, and children are raised, not educated.* *

*Allan Bloom, *The Closing of the American Mind* (New York: Simon & Schuster, 1987), p. 57.

# 11.

# WHICH WAY AHEAD? (A FEW MODEST PROPOSALS)

*Ideals basic to western democracies, such as equality and free-dom, have had a corrosive effect on the father-involved family. Christianity too has not always been as supportive of the biological family as it might be, due to its preoccupation with the needs of the spiritual family. The contemporary family crisis is forcing us to reconsider what biblical tradition might contribute to the recovery of a high culture of fathering.*

The exceptional fragility of the father-involved family in North America today may have roots that go deeper into our cultural history than we realize. Some researchers believe that the contemporary crisis of the family can be traced back to the writings of the seventeenth-century philosopher John Locke, whose ideas laid the foundations for the beginnings of democracy on this continent. In his treatises on government, Locke sought to undermine the divine right of kings by challenging the traditional role of fathers in families. His argument was that the very notion of special or privileged paternal power was suspect. Since the mother "has an equal title" to that of the father, he wrote, we should speak of *parental* power instead.[1] He went on to suggest that paternal power belongs so little to the father by some "peculiar right of Nature" that when he quits his care of his children "he loses power over them...." He saw the truth of this insight being verified "in those parts of America where, when the

127

husband and the wife part, which happens frequently, the children are all left to the mother...."[2] For Locke, in other words, the insight that paternal power is weak and without support in "Nature" becomes an argument for its overthrow! "At least from that time to the present," writes the religious psychologist David Bakan of Locke's philosophical critique of patriarchy, "the centrality of the family organization has been declining."[3]

This suggests that the intellectual climate of our western democracies may be more hostile to family values than is sometimes realized. "Freedom" and "equality" (the watchwords of our democratic culture) are not adequate categories for grasping what is going on or needed in this realm. While fathers and mothers are both parents, their "titles" (to use Locke's expression) are not equal, and a too great stress on personal freedom is destructive of the very foundations upon which the two-parent family is built. I refer again to the elementary fact that fathers, biologically speaking, are marginal to the reproductive process. It is the mothers who become pregnant and give birth; it is they who nurse at the breast. Since *nature* invests mothers with such power and preeminence in the human life-cycle, *culture* must intervene on behalf of fathers if they are to be equally (and as significantly) involved. The legal, religious, social and psychological means by which societies have done this have varied from culture to culture. But any civilization that fails to do *something* in this regard will inevitably witness the demise of the father-involved family and a drift toward families headed by mothers alone—precisely as John Locke observed, and as we see happening in America today to an unprecedented degree.[4]

Until recently the spiritual and emotional soil that nourished the father-involved family on the North American continent was the Bible. My intention in these essays has been to heighten the awareness of how these biblical traditions have and still can foster a high culture of fathering. My hope is that by regaining a better perspective on the way "biblical faith and fatherhood" intersect, we will be encouraged and empowered to continue to appropriate the insights of this tradition in support of contemporary family values.

With this in mind I will conclude with a few suggestions directed to Christians in particular for doing just that. What does a study of the fathering traditions of the Bible contribute to our current struggles in this regard?

## A Few Modest Proposals

One of the more important consequences of the research done in the preparation of the essays of this volume for me personally has been the dawning realization of the degree to which early Christianity, in breaking free of its Jewish moorings, tended to deemphasize the importance of the biological family in favor of the spiritual family (see Chapter 7). It was this shift in part, no doubt, that enabled Christianity to succeed so magnificently as a missionary religion within and beyond the boundaries of Judaism. Through its evangelism Christianity brought the spiritually homeless into spiritual families headed by spiritual fathers and God as father. In this way the legacy of biblical faith was spread far and wide.

In the process, however, were the needs of biological families neglected? Did Christianity in its break with Judaism lose something in this regard which was never fully recovered? Have, for example, Christians ever found an adequate substitute for the abandoned rituals of circumcision, redemption of the first born, or Passover? Of course, alternative family-related rituals were fashioned such as baptism and Eucharist. Baptism and Eucharist, however, are rituals of the church presided over by priests or pastors, not rituals of the family presided over by the father. It is doubtful therefore that these rituals perpetuate that link between faith and fatherhood that is such a novel feature of Hebraic biblical tradition.

Right here, it seems to me, might be one of the reasons why the Christian church is as vulnerable as it has been to the modern crisis of the family. Being aware of this weakness (if such it is) may be a first step in recovering a richer tradition of support for the father-involved family.

## Strengths

With these comments I do not mean to suggest that Christianity has neglected the family. This is obviously not the case. There are many ways in which Christians have been supportive of fathering. These strengths need to be identified, retained and enhanced. The following are a few examples of what I have in mind:

(1) Most Christians still do direct their worship to a God named and thought of as gracious all-powerful father. We still pray, "Our Father, hallowed be thy name...." I hope these essays will have encouraged those who want to uphold this tradition of worship in the face of pressures to do otherwise. I join Diane Tennis in urging: "Do not abandon God the Father....A reliable Father God is a source of judgment on unreliable sexual arrangements, a source of hope for women and for the fatherless, a symbol emerging out of our loss, luring itself in to existence."[5]

(2) Another strength of the churches so far as fathering is concerned is its teaching about sex and marriage, and its many wonderful marriage rituals and ceremonies. Let us guard against every tendency to weaken these teachings and traditions. Let us keep on warning of the dehumanizing consequences of sexual relating outside of a permanent lifelong marital commitment. Let us call upon men to be Christlike in their roles as husbands in their homes (Eph 5:25) and upon women to be respectful of their husbands in this role (Eph 5:33). Let us plead for the rights of children to grow up in the atmosphere of such bonded, caring, covenanted two-parent families.

(3) We still do value children and symbolize this in various ways in the church: by our sacred ceremonies for infants; by the way we bring children with us to our worship assemblies; by sitting together as families; by our Sunday schools; by our youth ministries, summer camps and the support given to para-church organizations like Boy and Girl Scouts; by our alternative schools, church-related high schools and colleges. All this is important and should be vigorously retained and promoted.

(4) Fathering is still highly regarded among us. A day for the honoring of fathers has been added to one honoring mothers in the annual cycle of fifty-two Sundays. Let us be vigilant in the use of this and other occasions to highlight the importance of fathers and fathering. "Fathering is a mark of a redeemed community," writes Diane Tennis. "The Christian community is without excuse for contributing to the absence or perversions of fathering. The Christian community must at minimum reorder its own life to give priority to fathering."[6] It is Theodore Stoneberg's conviction that

"The overarching task for the twenty-first century is to reconnect manhood and fatherhood in the lives of western men."[7]

(5) I lamented above the absence of rituals of the family in Christian tradition, but there is one tradition that is still alive in many Christian homes that might qualify as such, and that is the practice of prayer before meals. Fast foods and the pace of modern life are eroding the quality of our mealtimes. Nevertheless, we still do eat together, and as we do, let us be sure to keep this tradition alive. I would urge fathers especially to take a leadership role at this point and not let the responsibility for mealtime prayers fall by default to wives or children, as I have sometimes seen happening.

## Weaknesses

There are also areas of weakness, I sense—needs that are not being met, or at least not being met nearly as well as they might be. The following are a few thoughts about gaps in the parental support-systems of our churches that have come to mind in the course of writing these essays.

(1) Existent church rituals need to be studied to see how they could be shaped and made more explicitly supportive of parenting roles in the family, the role of the father especially. In Christian marriage ceremonies, for example, little reference is usually made to the roles of husbands and wives as parents. Even in our child dedication ceremonies we tend to focus more on the child than on parental tasks and responsibilities. William Johnson Everett suggests in his book on this subject that in addition to wedding ceremonies we need rituals that will help couples envision the parental role as a spiritual vocation—some public declaration of parental intentions, celebrated and solemnized at the time of the birth of a couple's first child, perhaps.[8]

(2) A ritual for children entering the teenage years may be useful. In a provocative book, *Momism, The Silent Disease of America,* Hans Sebold points to the dearth in American culture of rituals marking the transition from childhood to adulthood, such as the Jewish bar mitzvah.[9] The church of which I am a part fashioned such a ritual for its youth some years ago. These "teen-entry" celebrations, as we call them, bring together family

and friends to rejoice, reminisce and reflect about what lies ahead in the near and more distant future of the young person. Skits are often used for this part. A Bible is given, scriptures are read (the story of Jesus at twelve), songs are sung, prayers are offered, but it is not a religious commitment that is being celebrated on this occasion. It is merely recognizing that a new and important stage of life has arrived, the threshold of adulthood, when youth will more and more be responsible for the decisions and direction of their lives. The church and family are saying, "We wish you well and will stand by you."

(3) Another need in our churches, I sense, is for some quite specific guidance for fathers regarding what they are responsible for in the family (a document not unlike the one in the Jewish Talmud noted in Chapter 7). In a book entitled *Mothers Are People Too,* Anita Spencer seeks to develop just such an outline of duties for both fathers and mothers. Following the lead of Hans Sebold she calls them "A Healthy Motherhood Script" and "A Healthy Fatherhood Script."[10] In her "Healthy Fatherhood Script" she includes such items as genuine willingness to extend fathering, active involvement in home chores, and educational preparation for the father role. Various similar values are being promoted by organizations such as Focus on the Family, Promise Keepers, the National Fatherhood Initiative and the Institute for American Values. These developments are a hopeful sign that a new day may be dawning in the churches and culture so far as the father-involved family is concerned.[11]

## Concluding Comments

It should not be assumed, however, that the crisis of fatherlessness now confronting us in North America will be easily surmounted. Harvard University researcher Samuel Osherson, in a provocative book entitled *Finding Our Fathers: The Unfinished Business of Manhood,* writes that the interviews he has had with men in their thirties and forties have convinced him "that the psychological or physical absence of fathers from their families is one of the great underestimated tragedies of our times."[12] As I worked on the final draft of this volume, I chanced upon the following passage in Allan Bloom's highly acclaimed study, *The Closing of the American Mind:*[13]

> The fact that there is today a more affirmative disposition toward childbearing does not imply that there is any natural impulse or compulsion to establish anything like a traditional fatherhood to complement motherhood....Ninety per cent or more of children of divorced parents stay with their mothers, whose preeminent stake in children has been enhanced by feminist demands and by a consequent easy rationalization of male irresponsibility. So we have reproduction without family—if family includes the presence of a male who has any kind of a definite function. The return to motherhood as a feminist ideal is only possible because feminism has triumphed over the family as it was once known, and women's freedom will not be limited by it. None of this means returning to family values or even bodes particularly well for the family as an institution....

I must reluctantly agree with this somber analysis. And yet, along with others, I continue to hope that the tide might be turned, for it is altogether certain that should the father-involved family continue to disintegrate as it has over these past several decades, we will face increasingly unmanageable emotional and social disorders and our civilization will repeat the tragic pattern of decline and fall that so many others, for similar reasons, have experienced.[14]

# APPENDICES

# A BIBLICAL CHARTER
# OF CHILDREN'S RIGHTS:
# GENESIS 22

Jewish tradition refers to the story told in Genesis 22 as "the binding of Isaac," and regards it as a work of art and theological insight of a very high order, a classic of the rank of Jesus' parable of the lost son. Regarding it the noted biblical scholar E. A. Speiser has written (in his Genesis commentary) that it records "perhaps the profoundest personal experience in all recorded history and the telling of it rises to comparable literary heights."[1] In its opening line it refers to God "testing" Abraham as to whether he would be willing to offer up his son as a blood sacrifice, but what follows hints at something far greater: Abraham's step by step personal transformation, culminating in the revelation that this was not what God wanted of him after all.

It was not, then, Abraham's willingness to offer up his son, in and of itself, that is the focus of this account (in that respect Abraham was simply a child of his time), but the whole process by which he responded to this "test" and finally arrived at the point where it could be revealed to him that his prior understanding of what God wanted of him was faulty. Sacrificing a child was not the will of heaven. Within the culture of the time this was a momentous breakthrough. It still is.

In the comments that follow I seek to make transparent the epochal significance of this text. Its subtlety is already hinted at in the opening command to sacrifice Isaac. This summons is less straightforward than it might appear at first sight. To implement the blood sacrifice of his son, Abraham was asked to make a journey to a distant, unspecified location

137

(to "one of the mountains which I shall point out to you"). This meant he would have to travel. Time would elapse, time for certain things to occur.

This sets the stage for the narrative to unfold in progressive stages: first, the preparations for the journey; then the journey itself, culminating on the third day at the base of the mount where the sacrifice was to be made; then the climactic final events associated with the attempted human sacrifice.

## *1. Preparations*

In preparing for the journey Abraham is portrayed as rising early in the morning and setting promptly to work. He does not appear to want to waste a moment implementing the dreadful command that has come to him. Firewood is chopped, an ass is saddled, Isaac and two servants are summoned and the trek to the place of the sacrifice is begun. No words are spoken, no explanations given. The mother, Sarah, is strangely absent—not a hint that she even knew of the dreadful deed that Abraham was now contemplating. A sullen, intense silence hovers over this opening scene.

The British psychiatrist Erich Wellisch, in a sensitive psychological study of this episode,[2] characterizes Abraham during this phase of his ordeal as in a state of moral masochism, as when a father punishes a child. In clinical practice, he writes, fathers are observed who though ostensibly loving toward their sons turn against them with a vengeance. This change, although possibly in preparation for a long time, may occur suddenly, together with an urge for action that seems to be energized by a fanatical sense of necessity to do what is right.

> The moral quality of this power may become particularly obvious if the son's behaviour arouses the father's demand for punishment, as in the case of a teacher whose son falls short in his scholastic achievements, or of a preacher who discovers that his son has misbehaved sexually.
> The father may then turn against his son with a severity which is out of proportion to his son's actual misbehaviour. He attacks him in righteous indignation and with the conviction that he is directed to do so by the highest moral law. But closer observations may reveal that he does so with a heavy heart and that he is at least

as much, if not more, distressed about his own attitude against his son as about his son's failure....But at the same time he is bewildered about the apparently moral call in him which orders him to be severe with his son. He is in a state of moral masochism.[3]

It is on this note that the testing of Abraham opens, Wellisch suggests.

## 2. The Third Day

This awful silence between father and son persists until the third day of their journey, when the second act of this drama opens. Then it was, as they approached the place appointed by God for the sacrifice, that Abraham lifted up his eyes and saw it from afar, as in a vision. This third day experience was regarded in Jewish tradition as being of such tremendous importance that it was thought to have occurred on the first day of the month of Tischri, on Rosh-Hashanah the New Year's Day, when God will judge everything. In another tradition the third day of Abraham's journey coincided with Yom Kippur, the Day of Atonement.

At last Abraham speaks, first to his servants, then to his son, and for the first time we are privy to what is going on inside of him, in his heart.

To the servant he says that they should remain with the ass while he and "the boy" (he calls him) go yonder to worship and return again (22:5). Even now he does not tell his son what he is really intent upon doing. Nor is there any reference here to a divine command. Is this a hint that something inside of him is changing—that his moral masochism is weakening, that he is beginning to doubt the righteousness of what he is contemplating doing?

Then we are told how Abraham, still silent, took the wood for the burnt offering and loaded it on his son, while keeping the fire and the knife. With that the two of them went forward, it is reported (in a phrase repeated at the close of this scene), "the two of them...together" (22:6, 8).

Now at last father and son speak to each other. It is the son who takes the initiative ("Isaac spoke to his father Abraham..."). To do so he also had a "testing" to surmount, for he too had been silent to this point, perhaps out of fear or dread of what he imagined his father was about to do. Father and son, Wellisch writes of this and the following scene, were in process of saving each other.[4]

"Father?"

"Yes, my son," Abraham replied.

For the first time Abraham speaks *to* his son and calls him "my son." It is an emotional moment.

"Look,...here are the fire and the wood," Isaac asks (he does not mention the knife), "but where is the lamb for a burnt offering?" Isaac still has no inkling, apparently, of the dark thoughts that have been occupying his father during the three days they have been on the road together.

"My son, God himself will provide the lamb for the burnt offering," Abraham replies. This is now the second time he uses these magic words, "my son."

"And the two of them went on together" (22:8).

## 3. Final Events

Scene three takes place on the mountain appointed for the sacrifice (22:9–18). An altar is built and the wood arranged. Abraham binds his son and puts him on the altar on top of the wood. The sentences come swiftly. We marvel that Isaac utters no words of protest, nor resists his father in any way.

It is this moment especially that has gripped the imagination of generations of readers and prompted the caption "The Binding of Isaac." Abraham's power over his son is now absolute. The son's submission is equally absolute. All is now ready for the father to kill his son. The altar, the wood, the son, the knife, the fire, and, above all, the divine mandate—all are in place.

"Abraham had the right and the power to use the sword," Wellisch summarizes, "but he did not use it."[5] Why? Only because a revelation from on high broke through to his consciousness: "*Do not lay your hand on the lad or do anything to him;* for now I know that you fear God, seeing you have not withheld your son, your only son, from me."

At that moment, we are told, Abraham saw a lamb providentially caught in a thicket behind him and offered it instead. Then he called the name of that place: "Yahweh provides" (22:14).

The epochal significance of this story is epitomized by Wellisch in the following words:

> As the first of the great patriarchs of the Bible Abraham initiated a new era in the patriarchal order of the world....Love was the principle of the matriarchal order which ruled the world before the patriarchal principle of authority came into being. Abraham, by uniting authority with love, became the creator of the history of Israel.[6]

## Concluding Comments

The story recorded in Genesis 22 marks a turning point in the history of the father-involved family. Here at last is a father fully conscious that "heaven" does not want his children abused in a manner to which the cultures of antiquity had become accustomed. Through this story, for the first time in history so far as we know, the absolute power of fathers over their offspring was challenged and they were admonished in no uncertain terms not to harm their children—not to sacrifice them on the altar of their moral masochism.[7] As such Genesis 22 may be regarded as a charter of children's rights, a gift from antiquity for every family on earth.

# EPILOGUE

by Eugene R. August,

author of *The New Men's Studies: A Selected and Annotated Interdisciplinary Bibliography*

## Fatherhood and Men's Studies

When I completed *The New Men's Studies: A Selected and Annotated Interdisciplinary Bibliography,*[1] in 1994, I received a number of requests from the media to pick the "top ten" or the "twenty most important" books from the more than 1,000 books described in the bibliography. Although I declined making these selections in public (I would have slighted too many good books if I had), I found myself drawing up my own private list of the most significant books in the new bibliography. Among my personal "top ten" books was John W. Miller's *Biblical Faith and Fathering: Why We Call God "Father".*[2]

My reasons for selecting Miller's book are too many to enumerate here, and readers of this new edition will readily discover their own grounds for admiring it. But three of my reasons can be briefly mentioned. First, Miller dramatically challenged the prevailing orthodoxy in academia about God-talk, biblical patriarchy, and the history of fatherhood. Above all, he questioned the trendy belief that fatherhood is expendable. Second, although it took courage to argue as Miller did, it took genuine graciousness to present his arguments without the rancor that scars so much discussion of gender and religion. Despite the controversial territory it covered, Miller's book consistently radiated

Christian good will. Finally, there was the writing itself. As an English professor dismayed by the floods of gobbledygook unleashed by post-modernist discourse, I rejoiced at Miller's clarity of expression. By writing in a prose accessible to general readers, Miller performed that most democratic of tasks, that is, inviting as wide an audience as possible to participate in the dialogue about faith and fathers.

It is a pleasure to know that Paulist Press is publishing a new edition of Miller's superb book, and it is an honor for me to contribute to it a discussion of contemporary men's studies and fatherhood.

## Men's Studies

When one reviews the men's studies scholarship relating to fathers and fatherhood since the 1960s, several major observations can be made.

• The sheer volume of books and articles about fathers has grown considerably. In older studies of the family, father was often "the forgotten parent"; that is no longer true.

• This literature exhibits a wide spectrum of responses to fathers and fatherhood, ranging from father-hatred to father-hunger.

• Numerous studies demonstrate the great benefits of good (or "good enough") fathering to children, women, and men. Conversely, bad fathering or father-absence can produce devastating results for all concerned.

• *Contra* admirers of the single-parent family, evidence from the social sciences increasingly supports what Henry B. Biller calls "the two-parent advantage" that benefits children and parents alike.[3]

• Mounting evidence suggests that the good father may be a disappearing species. Many features of modern society subvert fatherhood, and fewer and fewer men seem willing or able to undertake the role of good family man.

• More recent studies and commentaries reflect a growing concern that many present-day social problems are rooted in fatherlessness.

• Finally, a number of "untouchable" topics related to fatherhood are presently avoided in public and academic discourse.

This epilogue discusses each of these facets of men's studies concerning fatherhood and broaches some of the "unmentionable" topics related to it.

But, first, a few words about "men's studies." This term refers to gender-conscious study of males as males, of masculinity as a social construction built upon a biological foundation, and of men's cultural and social issues. Men's studies is thus the necessary complement of women's studies: both are forms of gender studies, and there are two genders.

Over the past twenty years, the movement of men's studies into higher education has been slow but steady. Although men's studies has achieved nothing like the presence of women's studies on campuses, the number of men's studies courses offered at U.S. universities has increased from thirty in 1980 to over four hundred in 1997. The first men's studies program was created in 1997 at Hobart and William Smith Colleges, and a few other universities are planning to follow suit. The modest *Men's Studies Newsletter,* founded in 1984, evolved in 1992 into a full-fledged academic periodical, *The Journal of Men's Studies.* An American Men's Studies Association now flourishes. At scholarly conventions, panels on men's studies have been commonplace since the early 1980s, and nowadays entire conferences devoted solely to men's studies occur regularly. Above all, the increase in publication of gender-conscious men's studies has been extraordinary.

## Men's Studies and Fatherhood

In this literature, Father is a central, recurring figure. Not so long ago, however, he was "the forgotten parent" largely overlooked by social scientists. "Psychology has a long history of ignoring fathers," Ross D. Parke writes,[4] and the same could be said of other disciplines. The authors of a 1958 study titled *The Changing American Parent,* for example, interviewed 582 mothers and no fathers.[5] In 1979 Mel Roman and William Haddad in *The Disposable Parent* were still protesting that professional studies equated "mother" and "parent" and that "these studies only discover what their authors believe—that the father has no real importance."[6]

In sharp contrast, in 1997 all the contributors to a book titled *The Role of the Father in Child Development* routinely accepted the idea that fathers are critically important in family life.[7]

Still, academia does not treat fathers equally. The abundance of women's studies programs and the corresponding scarcity of men's studies courses (much less programs) ensure that the study of mothers will receive greater funding and attention than the study of fathers. The tendency of some colleges to view "Family Studies" as a branch of women's studies further diminishes paternity in these studies. Moreover, the prevailing liberal ideology of the academy includes the belief that alternate forms of family (especially the father-optional family) can substitute easily for the traditional father-mother family. As a result, many academics readily endorse the fatherless family and, as a consequence, devalue fatherhood. Some lesbian and gay activists on campuses target the father as an unnecessary and unwanted parent. Fathers have come a long way in academia but have a long way to go.

Indeed, fear and loathing of fathers and fatherhood has been fairly commonplace in men's studies, whether in academic writings or social commentaries. Much of the scholarly animosity directed against patriarchy as the evil empire masks a thinly veiled hostility to men in general and fathers in particular. In numerous publications since the late 1960s *patriarchy* is almost always an entirely negative term describing a tyranny of male domination over women, with "father rule" as the mark of women's oppression. "Patriarchy is the power of the fathers," writes Adrienne Rich, "a familial-social, ideological, political system in which men—by force, direct pressure, or through ritual, tradition, law, and language, customs, etiquette, education, and the division of labor—determine what part women shall or shall not play, and in which the female is everywhere subsumed under the male."[8] For many gender feminist writers, the "patriarchal family" is the site of female and child oppression, with father as the chief tyrant. Given the widespread endorsement of this view of fatherhood among educators, it is revolutionary and refreshing when John Miller defines the patriarchal family as the father-involved family and argues that this kind of family, warts and all, bestows irreplaceable benefits upon society.[9]

Often, patriphobic writings reflect a Marxist-based ideology, which may or may not be overtly expressed. Jeff Hearn, however, is forthright in announcing the Marxist grounding of his father-hatred: in *The Gender of Oppression: Men, Masculinity, and the Critique of Marxism,* Hearn calls for the abolition of fatherhood and urges men to become "sons within a possible matriarchy."[10] Intriguingly, in *Birth and Afterbirth: A Materialist Account,*[11] Hearn struggles with his own powerful feelings as a father and his belief that fatherhood is part of patriarchy's oppression of women. "Most importantly," he writes, "the notion of fatherhood must be smashed or more precisely dropped bit by bit into the ocean."[12]

The Marxian belief that the patriarchal family is at the root of most human evils dates back at least to Friedrich Engels' *The Origin of the Family, Private Property and the State,* first published in 1884.[13] Engels believed that the male oppression of women and the capitalist oppression of workers had a common origin in the founding of the patriarchal family. Although anthropologists no longer take Engels seriously as an historian of the family or society, his polemics against fatherhood still resonate in numerous ideologically-based attacks on patriarchy, the patriarchal family, fathers, and men.

Directly opposed to this view of fathers is another view which designates the idea of fathering as *the* essential component of civilization. One of the most influential accounts of this view is found in Margaret Mead's 1949 classic study, *Male and Female.*[14] In a chapter titled "Human Fatherhood is a Social Invention" Mead writes: "In every known society, everywhere in the world, the young male learns that when he grows up, one of the things he must do in order to be a full member of society is to provide food for some female and her young."[15] This socialization of males can be lost, Mead warns, if society does not conscientiously reinforce it. When this failure is allowed to happen, the society declines. Similar conclusions emerge in more recent studies. In *Manhood in the Making* (1990), David D. Gilmore finds that, almost universally, the norms of masculinity include protecting and providing for women and children.[16] Such studies suggest that fatherhood, far from being the origin of human evils, is the essence of a social order that benefits women and children, centers the lives of men, and maximizes the society's survival potential.

Attacks on fatherhood, however, also stem from some authors who are loosely characterized as "feminist" but who are more accurately described as lesbian-separatist. It goes without saying, one hopes, that all lesbian women are not separatist, misandric, or patriphobic; most likely, only a minority can be so described. Still, that minority exercises considerable authority in academia. The enormously influential writings of authors such as Mary Daly, Kate Millett, Dale Spender, and Adrienne Rich are laced with hostility toward heterosexuality, men, and fatherhood.[17] None of these authors conveys a positive vision of heterosexual relationships, much less of father-child relationships. "The mother-child relationship is the essential human relationship," writes Rich. "In the creation of the patriarchal family, violence is done to this fundamental human unit."[18] Not all patriphobes are women-centered women: John Stoltenberg's *Refusing to be a Man* might well be retitled *Refusing to be a Father.*[19] In short, the political platforms of some (but by no means all) gay activists contain an anti-paternal plank.

In striking contrast to this father-hatred is the widespread phenomenon of father-hunger. For many writers, men and women alike, the problem nowadays is not too much father but not enough father. Robert Bly's 1990 best seller *Iron John*[20] made "father-hunger" a nationally recognized term for a need as old as human history: even a cursory reading of Homer's *Odyssey* will locate father-hunger as one of the epic's principal themes. The son's search for a father is a staple of many early literatures, as in *Where the Two Came to Their Father,* a Diné-Navaho tale of twin boys who leave their mother and seek their father in order to become adult men.[21] In twentieth century studies, father-hunger has been a recurring theme over the years. Everett S. Ostrovsky's *Children Without Men*[22] explored the theme in 1962, and Richard Louv's *Father Love: What We Need, What We Seek, What We Must Create*[23] eloquently updates it in the 1990s. The father-hunger experienced by daughters is a more recent subject. Of studies examining the impact of good and bad fathering upon girls and women, Victoria Secunda's *Women and Their Fathers: The Sexual and Romantic Impact of the First Man in Your Life*[24] is notable for equitableness and fullness.

Long before the term "father-hunger" emerged, many studies were exploring the great impact of fathers and father absence upon children. An important early example is Leonard Benson's *Fatherhood: A Sociological Perspective* (1968),[25] significant not only for its determination to focus on fathers but also for its sympathetically enlightened approach to them. Scholars in many disciplines have since followed Benson's lead, and we now have a much more thoroughly documented understanding of the irreplaceable value of good fathering and the potentially crushing impact of bad fathering and father absence. Initially, the effect of the absent father upon children captured scholarly attention, but more recent studies have focused on the interaction of the "attached" father with his children and spouse. Increasingly, scholars are also attempting to study fatherhood in different cultures and to examine "nontraditional" fathers, such as gay fathers. Admirable summaries of current findings in these and other areas can be found in the third edition of *The Role of the Father in Child Development*, edited by Michael E. Lamb.[26]

Among the many topics that scholars have examined are the bonding of fathers and infants (hitherto believed to be almost non-existent), the decisive contributions of fathers to the child's intellectual, emotional, and spiritual well-being, and the usually negative effects of divorce and father absence on children. The long list of scholars who have contributed to this body of knowledge would have to include (at a bare minimum) Henry B. Biller, Martin Greenberg, Michael E. Lamb, James A. Levine, Robert A. Lewis, Ross D. Parke, and Frank A. Pedersen.[27] By 1981 Parke was able to summarize the findings of the new fatherhood literature:

> Fathers are no longer, if they ever were, merely a biological necessity. They are an important influence on their child's development. And a close relationship benefits the father as well as the child. Children need fathers, but fathers need their children too.[28]

Research since 1981 has confirmed and illuminated that conclusion.

The findings that link good fathering with child well-being have prompted several works of social commentary that connect fatherlessness with numerous social ills. The most thorough-going of these studies, David Blankenhorn's *Fatherless America,* traces many of America's social problems to ever-larger numbers of abandoning or exiled fathers.[29] Blankenhorn depicts the potential loss of fatherhood envisioned by Margaret Mead as becoming reality: America's failure to reinforce good fathering has produced a growing forgetfulness among men of how to father responsibly. To remedy this critical situation, Blankenhorn proposes twelve specific measures to help ensure that every child has a father.

## Unfinished Agenda

While the need for good fathering is becoming more evident in our national discourse, other matters relating to faith and fatherhood remain either under-discussed or off-limits to discussion altogether:

• Scholars and religious leaders have barely begun to address the question of how well traditional religions are meeting the needs of men, especially family men. Currently, many men seem alienated from organized religion as a "feminized" activity that has little relevance to masculine endeavors. In men's studies, mythopoetic spirituality predominates, and questions involving masculinity and traditional religions are left largely unexamined.

• Scholars and religious leaders have been reluctant to examine critically whether gender feminist appraisals of God-talk and God-images are valid. Too often, clergy and laity seem to have accepted these critiques largely to avoid appearing "sexist." Moreover, the assumption that God the Father can easily be replaced by, or accommodated to, more "inclusive" concepts of deity needs to be questioned closely. Certainly, John Miller's arguments on this point merit serious attention. Roman Catholic leaders, moreover, might well ask whether the shortage of priests (called "Fathers" by the laity) is related to the current disparagement of God-as-Father and of fatherhood itself.

• Although debate over legalized abortion has been raging for nearly three decades, precious little attention has been paid to whether abortion laws contribute to subverting fatherhood. Do laws that grant the mother the right to decide unilaterally whether an unborn child lives or dies send a signal to men that the child belongs to the mother, that the father is a secondary parent at best? Do such laws foster male detachment from children and thus promote male irresponsibility toward mother and child? Clearly, such questions will make the abortion debate more explosive than it is already, but they need to be asked.

• A host of issues connected with gay rights need to be considered in relation to fathers and fatherhood. For example, discussion of placing same-sex marriage on the same legal footing as heterosexual marriage needs to consider whether such a move will recognize the "father-optional" family as a legitimate and equivalent alternative to the "father-present" family. Would a legal recognition that "father is optional" further erode male commitment to responsible fatherhood? While working to eliminate the evil of gay-bashing in modern society, people of good will—straight and gay—also need to critique certain features of some gay agendas.

• Our society needs to stigmatize the widespread misandry in education, news media, and entertainment as a pernicious form of sex-hatred. In academia, male-bashing is *the* acceptable form of sexism, yet college activists never target it as one of the "hate crimes" to be eradicated from campuses. Often this misandry appears in stereotypes of fathers as dangerous and unreliable. Legitimate criticism of destructive paternal behaviors is one thing; wholesale father-trashing is quite another.

• The academic programs of most universities are now badly unbalanced in the area of gender studies and need to be adjusted. Compared with the ubiquitous women's studies, men's studies is rare on college campuses. The imbalance ensures that gender-conscious study of males and fatherhood will receive less than equitable attention among academics.

• The question of whether fatherhood is entirely a social invention needs to be examined more critically. Too many scholars in men's studies (and other areas of the humanities and the social sciences) seem unwarrantably committed to the notion that fatherhood is entirely a social "construction" with no biological basis.

• Terms such as *patriarchy, patriarchal society,* and *patriarchal family* badly need to be redefined and employed in a non-politicized context. At present, the word *patriarchy* seems to have little or no meaning except as an all-purpose smear term to bolster questionable theories of the universal oppression of women and children by "fathers." Responsible scholars need to insist that patriarchy be seen clearly in all its diversity, with its benefits and drawbacks equitably noted.

• Scholars and the general public need to note that the recent rise of goddess-worship is often fueled by misandry and patriphobia. Modern goddess-worship, moreover, frequently is rooted in suspect accounts of ancient matriarchies, which are usually depicted as idyllic societies destroyed by brutish patriarchs. Scholars need to critique such accounts and to challenge the sexism of beliefs that target fatherhood as the world's primary evil.

• And, finally, a larger question: If fatherhood is to be an option for a declining number of men in the future, what self-affirming and socially beneficial vocations will replace it? Does modern society need to develop a moral equivalent of fatherhood? Can it do so?

In these and other considerations, it would be well to bear in mind the words of Margaret Mead:

> The continuance of the [heterosexual two-parent] family to date, its re-establishment after catastrophe or ideological destruction, is not however a guarantee that this will always be the case, that our generation can relax and take it for granted that this will always be so.[30]

Increasingly, the challenge modern societies face is whether they can survive the loss of fatherhood.

# NOTES

## PREFACE TO THE FIRST EDITION

1. "In Defense of Monotheistic Father Religion," *The Journal of Religion and Health,* Spring 1983; "The Contemporary Fathering Crisis: The Bible and Research Psychology," *The Conrad Grebel Review,* Fall 1983; "God as Father in the Bible and the Father Image in Several Contemporary Ancient Near Eastern Myths: A Comparison," *Studies in Religion/Sciences Religieuses,* Summer 1985; "Departriarchalizing God in Biblical Interpretation: A Critique," *The Catholic Biblical Quarterly,* October 1986.

## PREFACE TO THE SECOND EDITION

1. For Nietzsche's comments in this regard, see my essay in Chapter 10.

2. For an overview and analysis of these developments, see especially David Blankenhorn, *Fatherless America, Confronting Our Most Urgent Social Problem* (New York: Basic Books, 1995); David Popenoe, *Life Without Father, Compelling New Evidence that Fatherhood and Marriage are Indispensable for the Good of Children and Society* (New York: Martin Kessler Books, The Free Press, 1996).

3. On the transition underway in our culture from a weakened to a deinstitutionalized family structure, and the challenges it poses, see Carl E. Schneider, "The Law and the Stability of Marriage: The Family as a Social Institution," in *Promises to Keep, Decline and Renewal of Marriage in America*, David Popenoe, Jean Bethke Elshtain and David Blankenhorn, eds. (Lanham: Rowman & Littlefield Publishers, 1996), pp. 187–213.

4. The outstanding exception is Don S. Browning, "Biology, Ethics, and Narrative in Christian Family Theory," in *Promises to Keep,* pp. 119–156; "Love, Christian Family Theory and Evolutionary Psychology," in *From Cultural Wars to Common Ground, Religion and the American Family*

*Debate*, Don S. Browning and Ian S. Evison, eds. (Louisville: Westminster John Knox Press, 1997), pp. 101–128. Browning writes of the "asymmetrical reproductive strategies of males and females" and of the consequent "male problematic" as this comes to light through an analysis of the "evolutionary ecology" of the male-headed household. This affords him insights and perspectives on biblical patriarchy that sets his work apart from that of his colleagues in the volumes he and Ian Evison have edited in *Families in Ancient Israel,* Leo G. Perdue, Joseph Blenkinsopp, John J. Collins, Carol Meyers (Louisville: Westminster John Knox Press, 1997), and *Families in the New Testament World,* Carolyn Osiek and David L. Balch (Louisville: Westminster John Knox Press, 1997). The latter seem oblivious of the issues and challenges involved in the emergence of "patricentric" families and cultures and hence tend to view them simply as "androcentric" and oppressive in the light of contemporary equalitarian ideals.

## 2. ORIGINS OF THE FATHER-INVOLVED FAMILY

1. These trends may be endemic to American culture. In *Prodigals and Pilgrims: The American Revolution against Patriarchal Authority, 1750–1800* (Cambridge: Cambridge University Press, 1982), p. 267, Jay Fliegelman states (and then develops) the thesis that "the American revolution against patriarchal authority in the second half of the eighteenth century provided the paradigm by which Americans for the next two hundred years would understand and set forth the claims of both individual and national independence." See my further comments on a related issue in Chapter 11.

2. Typical are Gerda Lerner's comments in *The Creation of Patriarchy* (New York: Oxford University Press, 1986), p. 238, where she writes that "gender is a set of cultural roles. It is a costume, a mask, a straitjacket in which men and women dance their unequal dance." On the manner in which this issue intrudes into the very center of feminist theology, and its impact on contemporary feminist family theory and policies, see Chapter 10 of this volume.

3. For the statistical evidence, see Walter F. Horn, *Father-Facts,* Third Edition (The National Fatherhood Initiative, 1998), pp. 12f. According to U.S. governmental sources, "In 1995, nearly 19 million children lived with only one parent, and of these children 87% lived with their mother" (p. 12).

4. For a sampling of this research see David Popenoe, *Life Without Father, Compelling New Evidence That Fatherhood and Marriage are Indispensable for the Good of Children and Society* (New York: The Free Press, 1996); also

the essays (36 in all) in *Father and Child, Developmental and Clinical Perspectives,* Stanley Cath, et al. (Boston: Little, Brown, 1982).

5. Blankenhorn, *Fatherless America,* p. 76, traces the astonishing change of mind that has occurred in North American society since 1992 regarding the actual need for a father in the home. He reports that "a recent survey finds that fully 70 percent of younger Americans, age eighteen to thirty-four, now endorse the proposition that it is morally acceptable to have children outside of marriage" (p. 76).

6. For an earlier discussion of these issues, see my "The Contemporary Fathering Crisis: The Bible and Research Psychology," *The Conrad Grebel Review* (Fall 1983): 21–37 (reprinted in this volume; see Chapter 8).

7. See my "God as Father in the Bible and the Father Image in Several Contemporary Ancient Near Eastern Myths: A Comparison," *Studies in Religion/Sciences Religieuses* 14/3 (Summer 1985): 347–354 (reprinted in this volume; see Chapter 3).

8. The radical centrality of this way of naming God in biblical faith is the theme of my "Depatriarchalizing God in Biblical Interpretation: A Critique," *The Catholic Biblical Quarterly,* 48/4 (October 1986): 609–616 (reprinted in this volume; see Chapter 4).

9. David Bakan, *And They Took Themselves Wives: The Emergence of Patriarchy in Western Civilization* (San Francisco: Harper & Row, 1979); Peter Wilson, *Man the Promising Primate: The Conditions of Human Evolution,* second edition (New Haven: Yale University Press, 1983; first edition, 1980); Mary O'Brien, *The Politics of Reproduction* (London: Routledge & Kegan Paul, 1981); Don S. Browning, "Biology, Ethics, and Narrative in Christian Family Theory," in *Promises to Keep, Decline and Renewal of Marriage in America,* David Popenoe, Jean Bethke Elshtain, and David Blankenhorn, eds. (Lanham: Rowan & Littlefield, 1996), pp. 119–156.

10. O'Brien, *ibid.,* p. 21, calls attention to "the strong historical tendency" to suppress this discovery and see reproduction instead as " 'pure' biological process...without mind; irrational or at least pre-rational."

11. Bronislaw Malinowski, *The Father in Primitive Psychology* (New York: W. W. Norton, 1927).

12. *Ibid.,* p. 12.

13. Data bearing on this discovery is assembled by David Mace, *Hebrew Marriage: A Sociological Study* (London: The Epworth Press, 1953), pp. 205f.; Gerda Lerner, *The Creation of Patriarchy,* pp. 185–193; and Mary Lefkowitz and Maureen Fant, *Women's Life in Greece & Rome: A Source Book in*

*Translation* (Baltimore: Johns Hopkins Press, 1982), pp. 82–87. See also the further discussion of this issue in Chapter 3.

14. Gerda Lerner, *Creation of Patriarchy*, characterizes this development as the "appropriation by men of woman's sexual and reproductive capacity" (p. 8), and regards it as the critical event in the rise of "patriarchy" as she defines it (male domination of women). She does not seem to recognize that this step was essential to the emergence of the father-involved family as such. On this issue, see the research cited by David Popenoe, *Life without Father*, p. 175, pointing to the critical role of "paternity confidence" in the emergence of the father-involved family. He writes that "some evolutionists believe that high paternal investments evolved only after monogamy had produced increased paternity confidence."

15. Bakan, *And They Took Themselves Wives*, p. 14, refers to this as the "effeminization of the male. In coming to share the care of children, he came to share in the archaic function of the female."

16. Peter Wilson, *Man the Promising Primate*, p. 71.

17. Regarding these modern developments, see especially Alexander Mitscherlich, *Society Without the Father: A Contribution to Social Psychology* (New York: Harcourt, Brace & World, 1963; English translation, 1969), and Edward Shorter, *The Making of the Modern Family* (New York: Basic Books, 1975).

18. The way, for example, the typical Greek father of antiquity neglected his wife and children (and the consequences of this) are fully documented by Philip Slater, *The Glory of Hera: Greek Mythology and the Greek Family* (Boston: Beacon Press, 1968); for similar problems in African society, see H. Collomb and S. Valantin, "The Black African Family," in J. Anthony and C. Koupernik, eds., *The Child in His Family* (New York: J. Wiley, 1970), pp. 359–388; for India, see Sudhir Kakar, "Father and Sons: An Indian Experience," in Stanley Cath, et al., eds, *Father and Child* (Boston: Little, Brown, 1982), pp. 417–442; for China, Japan, and other examples, see the summaries in David Lynn, *The Father*, pp. 33–44.

19. Regarding the severity of these rituals as this relates to the intensity of the mothering factor and the non-involvement of the fathers, see William N. Stephens, *The Oedipus Complex: Cross-Cultural Evidence* (New York: The Free Press of Glencoe, 1962).

20. The evidence bearing on fathering among the pre-hominid primates is summarized by Wilson, *Man the Promising Primate*, who states that "on the whole it can be said that most primate males are unable to identify their children"

(p. 48). Foreshadowings of a fathering role appear in a few lower species (wolves and gibbons are the notable examples); its absence, and the dominance instead of the mother among virtually all other sentient animals (and generally among primitive cultures) is thoroughly documented by Robert Biffault, *The Mother: The Matriarchal Theory of Social Origins* (New York: Macmillan, 1931).

21. "The myth breathes an atmosphere of unabashed sensuality," writes Samuel Terrien of this passage, in *Till the Heart Sing: A Biblical Theology of Manhood & Womanhood* (Philadelphia: Fortress Press, 1986), p. 16.

22. Helen Fisher, *The Sex Contract, The Evolution of Human Behavior* (New York: Quill, 1982), pp. 121f.

23. *Ibid.,* p. 145.

24. The highly complex nature of this achievement is the central theme of Wilson's *Man the Promising Primate.*

## 3. MALE-CENTERED REPRODUCTIVE BIOLOGY

1. In an essay on "Patriarchy," *Dictionary of Feminist Theologies,* eds. Letty M. Russell and J. Shannon Clarkson (Louisville: Westminster John Knox Press, 1996), Rosemary Radford Ruether writes that "*Patriarchy* means the 'rule of the father.' Patriarchy refers to systems of legal, social, economic, and political relations that validate and enforce the sovereignty of male heads of families over dependent persons in the household" (p. 205).

2. Gerda Lerner, *The Creation of Patriarchy* (New York: Oxford University Press, 1986), pp. 146–152; David Bakan, *And They Took Themselves Wives: The Emergence of Patriarchy in Western Civilization* (San Francisco: Harper & Row, 1979), p. 26; Ann Barstow, "The Prehistoric Goddess," in *The Book of the Goddess Past and Present: An Introduction to Her Religion,* Carl Olson, ed. (New York: Crossroad, 1985), pp. 7–15.

3. Quoted from Mary R. Lefkowitz and Maureen B. Fant, *Woman's Life in Greece & Rome: A Source Book in Translation* (Baltimore: Johns Hopkins University Press, 1982), p.84.

4. Lerner, *The Creation of Patriarchy,* p. 205.

5. *De Opificio Mundi,* p. 67, quoted from Ephraim Urbach, *The Sages* (Cambridge: Harvard University Press, 1987), p. 226.

6. David Mace, *Hebrew Marriage: A Sociological Study* (London: The Epworth Press, 1953), p. 206.

7. *Ibid.*

8. David Bakan, *And They Took themselves Wives*, pp. 27f.

9. "Thus," she writes, "the first appropriation of private property consists of the appropriation of the labor of women as *reproducers*" (Lerner, *Creation of Patriarchy*, p. 52).

10. *Ibid.*, p. 218.

11. "What will come after," she concludes, "what kind of structure will be the foundation for alternate forms of social organization we cannot yet know." *Ibid.*, p. 229. This issue remains unaddressed in Lerner's sequel volume, *The Creation of Feminist Consciousness, From the Middle Ages to Eighteen-Seventy* (New York: Oxford University Press, 1983).

12. See "Origins of the Father-Involved Family" (Chapter 2 in this volume).

13. For a review of family law in the Hammurabi Code and the Bible, see Hans Jochen Boecker, *Law and the Administration of Justice in the Old Testament and the Ancient East* (Minneapolis: Augsburg, 1980), pp. 100–122.

14. For an insightful discussion of this point, see David Mace, *Hebrew Marriage: A Sociological Study* (London: The Epworth Press, 1953), pp. 189–200.

15. See Helen E. Fisher, *The Sex Contract: The Evolution of Human Behavior* (New York: Quill, 1983), pp. 119–122, for fossil evidence of male participation in the family group as early as four million years ago.

16. For a summary of the Roman traditions and laws in this regard, see "The Patria Potestas," in William Barclay, *Train Up a Child* (Philadelphia: Westminster, 1959), pp. 267–270.

17. For a review of this tragic chapter of our human past (and the shadow it continues to cast over our present), see Erich Wellisch's book-length study, *Isaac and Oedipus. A Study in Biblical Psychology of the Sacrifice of Isaac: The Akedah* (Routledge & Kegan Paul, 1953); Michael Tooley, *Abortion and Infanticide* (Oxford: Clarendon Press, 1983); Alberto Ravinell and Whitney Green, *The Role of Human Sacrifice in the Ancient Near East* (Missoula: Scholars Press, 1975); Bernhard Erling, "First-Born and Firstlings in the Covenant Code," *Society of Biblical Literature Seminar Papers Series*, No. 25 (Atlanta: Scholars Press, 1986), pp. 470–490.

18. Wellisch's study, *Isaac and Oedipus*, seeks to highlight the uniqueness and importance of this event for the future of the father-involved family in human history generally.

19. The way a high culture of fathering flourished within the context of biblical faith, and why, is the focus of the essays in Parts III and IV of this volume.

## 4. GOD THE FATHER IN THE BIBLE AND A.N.E. MYTHS: A COMPARISON

1. Joseph Campbell, *The Hero with a Thousand Faces,* Bollingen Series XVII (Princeton: Princeton University Press, 1949), p. 19.

2. Philip Slater, *The Glory of Hera: Greek Mythology and the Greek Family* (Boston: Beacon Press, 1968), p. xvi.

3. According to E. O. James, *The Worship of the Sky-God: A Comparative Study in Semitic and Indo-European Religion* (University of London: The Athlone Press, 1963), p. 8, father deities tend to be *Deus otiosus* and marginal to the cult "everywhere in primitive states of culture both in the present and the past."

4. My thesis is thus almost the opposite of the one put forward by Naomi Goldenberg in *Changing of the Gods: Feminism and the End of Traditional Religions* (Boston: Beacon Press, 1979), p. 37, who writes that "all recorded history has been patriarchal" and that for the first time today (in the wake of the feminist movement) we are about to see "what happens when father-gods die for an entire culture...." The truth is (as I will try to show) that father gods were far from alive and well even in antiquity (also see n. 3 above).

5. In the analysis that follows, references are to the translation of this myth by E. A. Speiser, in *Ancient Near Eastern Texts,* ed. by James Pritchard (Princeton: Princeton University Press, 1955), pp. 60–72.

6. For an analysis of this epic as a story about resistances to growing up, see Thorkild Jacobson, *The Treasures of Darkness: A History of Mesopotamian Religion* (New Haven: Yale University Press, 1976), pp. 218–219.

7. For the sake of convenience, references in the following discussion are to the widely accessible translation of these myths by H. L. Ginsbert in *Ancient Near Eastern Texts* (see n. 6 above) where an older numbering system is used than the one now in vogue; see J. C. L. Gibson, *Canaanite Myths and Legends* (Edinburgh: T. & T. Clark, 1977).

8. For an English translation of Plutarch's rendering of these myths see J. Griffiths, *Plutarch's De Iside et Osiride: Edited with an Introduction, Translation and Commentary* (University of Wales Press, 1970).

9. Concerning the way this myth reflected and influenced father-son-mother relations in Egyptian society see Jan Assmann, "Das Bild des Vaters im alter Agpyten," in *Dad Vaterbild in Mythos and Geschichte,* ed. by Bornkamm, et al. (Stuttgart: Kohlhammer, 1976), pp. 24–27.

10. John Priest, "Myth and Dream in Hebrew Scripture," in *Myths, Dreams and Religion,* ed. by Joseph Campbell (New York: E. P. Dutton and Co., 1970), p. 55.

11. *Ibid.,* p. 56.

12. The pronoun "he" is very close to being a divine name in the expression "I am he" (Dt 32:39; Is 43:10; etc.), "you are he" (Ps 102:27). On this usage and the possible importance of "he" as an initial focus of cultic devotion in biblical religion, see S. Mowinckel, "The Name of the God of Moses," *Hebrew Union College Annual,* 33 (1961), pp. 121–133.

13. El is both the name of the Canaanite father deity and the generic term for god. Evidence pointing to a link between Canaanite El and the God of the Bible is reviewed by J. J. M. Roberts, "El," in *Interpreter's Dictionary of the Bible,* Supplementary Volume (Nashville: Abingdon, 1976), pp. 255–258. Concerning the representation of God as father in the Bible see Robert Hammerton-Kelly, *God the Father: Theology and Patriarchy in the Teaching of Jesus* (Philadelphia: Fortress Press, 1979).

14. The characterization of Yahweh as "jealous" is "the basic element in the whole OT idea of God," according to Walter Eichrodt, *Theology of the Old Testament,* vol. 1 (Philadelphia: Westminster Press, 1961), p. 210, n. 1.

15. The literature and arguments leading to this conclusion are reviewed by G. H. Parke-Taylor, *Yahweh: The Divine Name in the Bible* (Waterloo: Wilfrid Laurier Univ. Press, 1975), pp. 46–52.

16. *Ibid.,* pp. 60–61.

17. Concerning the central importance of this passage in Old Testament theology, see Brevard Childs, *The Book of Exodus: A Critical, Theological Commentary* (Philadelphia: Westminster, 1974), p. 615.

18. David Bakan, *And they Took Themselves Wives: The Emergence of Patriarchy in Western Civilization* (San Francisco: Harper & Row, 1979), p. 13.

19. *Ibid.*

20. Further to this point, see my "The Contemporary Fathering Crisis: The Bible and Research Psychology," *The Conrad Grebel Review,* Fall 1983, pp. 21–37 (Chapter 8 in this volume).

## 5. Depatriarchalizing God

1. Phyllis Trible, "Depatriarchalizing in Biblical Interpretation," *Journal of the American Academy of Religion* 41 (1973), pp. 30–48. For a review of feminist research on God symbolism, including that of Trible, see Carol Christ,

"Symbols of Goddess and God in Feminist Theology," in Carl Olsen, ed., *The Book of the Goddess Past and Present: An Introduction to Her Religion* (New York: Crossroad, 1983), pp. 231–251; Francis Martin, *The Feminist Question, Feminist Theology in the Light of Christian Tradition* (Grand Rapids: Eerdmans, 1994), pp. 221–264. Further to this issue, see also Chapter 10 of this volume.

2. Trible, "Depatriarchalizing," p. 31.

3. *Ibid.*, pp. 31, 48.

4. Phyllis Trible, "God, Nature of, in the OT," *The Interpreter's Dictionary of the Bible, Supplementary Volume* (Nashville: Abingdon Press, 1976), pp. 368–369; see also her essays in *God and the Rhetoric of Sexuality, Overtures to Biblical Theology* (Philadelphia: Fortress, 1978).

5. For a critique of biblical patriarchy based on this assumption, see Sallie McFague, *Metaphorical Theology: Models of God in Religious Language* (Philadelphia: Fortress, 1982), pp. 145–177.

6. The analysis here is that of religious psychologist Antoine Vergote. See especially his essays, "The Parental Figures: Symbolic Functions and Medium for the Representation of God," and "Overview and Theoretical Perspective," chs. 1 and 8, in *The Parental Figures and the Representation of God: A Psychological and Cross-Cultural Study*, eds. Antoine Vergote and Alvero Tamayo (The Hague/Paris/New York: Mouton, 1981) 13, pp. 186, 220.

7. *Ibid.*, pp. 195–196. See also Vergote's discussion of these issues in his *The Religious Man: A Psychological Study of Religious Attitudes* (Dublin: Gill and Macmillan, 1969), pp. 143–200, and now more recently, David Gutmann, "The Paternal Imperative," *American Scholar* (Winter 1998), pp. 118–126. For excellent summaries of the research on fathering see the thirty-six essays in *Father and Child: Developmental and Clinical Perspectives,* eds. Stanley Cath, et al. (Boston: Little, Brown, 1982); *The Role of the Father in Child Development,* ed. Michael Lamb, third edition (New York: John Wiley, 1997).

8. *The Religious Man,* p. 177.

9. Vergote, *Parental Figures,* p. 220.

10. Further to this point see my "The Contemporary Fathering Crisis: The Bible and Research Psychology," *Conrad Grebel Review* 1 (Fall 1983), pp. 22–37 (Chapter 8 in this volume). Concerning the relatively "high status" of women in the Old Testament, see John H. Otwell, *And Sarah Laughed: The Status of Women in the Old Testament* (Philadelphia: Westminster, 1977); Hans Walter Wolff, *Anthropology of the Old Testament* (Philadelphia: Fortress, 1974), pp. 169–173.

11. "Depatriarchalizing," p. 32.

12. "God, Nature of, in the OT," p. 369.

13. *Ibid.*, p. 368.

14. *Ibid.*

15. *Ibid.*

16. *Ibid.*

17. On *ēl raḥûm* (Ex 34:6; Ps 86:15) as one example among many of Yahweh's "debt to El's Canaanite past," see J. J. M. Roberts, "El," *Interpreter's Dictionary of the Bible, Supplementary Volume,* p. 257.

18. For an analysis of the complex issues involved in establishing the etymology of this word see Frank Moore Cross, *Canaanite Myth and Hebrew Epic: Essays in the History of the Religion of Israel* (Cambridge: Harvard University, 1973), pp. 52–56.

19. *Ibid.*, p. 55.

20. For several additional suggestions see Virginia Ramey Mollenkott, *The Divine Feminine: The Biblical Imagery of God as Female* (New York: Crossroad, 1983).

21. Trible, "God, Nature of, in the OT," p. 368.

22. *God and Rhetoric of Sexuality, Overtures to Biblical Theology,* eds. Walter Brueggemann, John Donahue (Philadelphia: Fortress, 1978), pp. 12–23.

23. Trible, "Depatriarchalizing," p. 34.

24. On this point, see again J. J. M. Roberts, "El," pp. 255–258.

25. God is referred to as father twenty-one times in the Old Testament, two hundred and fifty-five times in the New Testament, according to Felix Donahue, "The Spiritual Father in the Scriptures," in *Abba: Guides to Wholeness and Holiness East and West,* ed. John R. Sommerfeldt (Kalamazoo: Cistercian, 1982), pp. 3, 6. Malachi is thus only stating the obvious when he asks: "Is there not one father of us all? Did not one God create us?" (Mal 2:10).

26. The literature and arguments leading to this conclusion are reviewed by G. H. Parke-Taylor, *Yahweh: The Divine Name in the Bible* (Waterloo: Wilfrid Laurier University, 1975), pp. 46–52.

27. Lk 11:2; Jn 17:6, 11, 12, 26.

28. Raphael Patai, *The Hebrew Goddess* (New York: Avon Books, 1967), p. 9.

## 6. New Modes of Human Fathering (Hebrew Scriptures)

1. The best review to date of human fathering in biblical tradition is the substantial essay by Lothar Perlitt, "Das Bild des Vaters im Alten Testament," in *Das Vaterbild in Mythos and Geschichte,* H. Tellenbach, ed. (Stuttgart: W.

Kohlhammer, 1976), pp. 50–101; but see also Roland de Vaux, *Ancient Israel, Its Life and Institutions* (London: Darton, Longman & Todd, 1961), pp. 19–55; E. S. Gerstenberger and W. Schrage, *Woman and Man, Biblical Encounters Series* (Nashville: Abingdon, 1980); James B. Hurley, *Man and Woman in Biblical Perspective* (Grand Rapids: Zondervan, 1981). On the "father centered" quality of "biblical psychology," see also Henry Abramovitch, "Images of the Father in Psychology and Religion," in *The Role of the Father in Child Development*, Michael E. Lamb, ed. (New York: John Wiley & Sons, third edition, 1997), pp. 19–32.

2. Regarding the expression "father and mother" and its centrality and pervasiveness in Israelite tradition, see Perlitt, "Das Bild des Vaters," pp. 60–62, where he writes: "So gibt es kaum eine Sphäre des Lebens, in der ein Israelit seiner Eltern anders gedächte als in der Gleichrangigkeit und ausdrücklichen Nennung von Vater *und* Mutter [Thus, there is hardly any sphere of life in which an Israelite thought of his parents otherwise than in terms of the equalizing and definitive terminology of father *and* mother]" (p. 61).

3. On the exodus narratives seen from this point of view, see the seminal study by Theodor Reik, *Mystery on the Mountain: The Drama of the Sinai Revelation* (New York: Harper & Brothers, 1959), and also my essay, "Psychoanalytic Approaches to Biblical Religion," *Journal of Religion and Health*, 22/1 (Spring 1983), pp. 19–29.

4. Regarding the importance of the story of Abraham's near sacrifice of Isaac for the future of the father-involved family, see Chapter 3 of this volume ("Male-Centered Reproductive Biology and the Dynamics of Biblical Patriarchalism"); also "A Biblical Charter of Children's Rights," in the Appendix.

5. In her study of Jewish child-rearing practices, Shoshana Matzner-Bekerman, *The Jewish Child: Halakhic Perspectives* (New York: KTAV Publishing House, 1984), discusses the ceremony of the "Redemption of the First-Born" (Chapter 4). My comments on contemporary practice are indebted to her description of this ceremony, pp. 56–59.

6. For a succinct, authoritative summary of what is known about this ritual from both biblical and extra-biblical sources, see Roland de Vaux, *Ancient Israel*, pp. 46–48.

7. Felix Bryk, *Circumcision in Man and Woman: Its History, Psychology and Ethnology* (New York: American Ethnological Press, 1934), pp. 181–187.

8. Roland de Vaux, *Ancient Israel*, p. 47.

9. *The Jewish Child*, pp. 45–51.

10. Regarding the important role that fathers play in the maturation of daughters as well as sons, see Chapters 8 and 9 in this volume.

11. William Barclay, *Train Up a Child: Educational Ideals in the Ancient World* (Philadelphia: Westminster, 1959). See also I. F. Dobson, *Ancient Education and Its Meaning to Us* (New York: Cooper Square Publishers, 1963); A. G. Beck, *Album of Greek Education: The Greeks at School and at Play* (Sydney: Cheiron Press, 1975); Stanley F. Bonner, *Education in Ancient Rome* (London: Methuen & Co., 1977).

12. The source of this quotation is Plutarch's *Cato Major* as quoted by Barclay, *Train Up a Child*, p. 155.

13. Jerome Carcopino, *Daily Life in Ancient Rome: The People and the City at the Height of the Empire* (New Haven and London: Yale University Press, 1940), p. 107.

14. Carol Meyers in "Procreation, Production, and Protection: Male-Female Balance in Early Israel," *Journal of the American Academy of Religion*, LI/4 (December 1983): 569–593, has assembled an array of archaeological and textual evidence pointing to a high degree of equality among men and women in Iron Age Israel. She believes that the account of the creation of woman in Genesis 2 was written to provide ideological support for this state of affairs. For an expanded version of this essay, see Carol Meyers, "The Family in Early Israel," in *Families in Ancient Israel*, Leo G. Perdue, Joseph Blenkinsopp, John J. Collins, Carol Meyers (Louisville: Westminster John Knox Press, 1997), pp. 1–47.

15. Walter Brueggemann makes a similar point in *The Creative Word: Canon as Model for Biblical Education* (Philadelphia: Fortress Press, 1982), p. 15. In the exchanges between parents and children alluded to in such texts as Exodus 12:26; 13:8, 14, Deuteronomy 6:20–21, and Joshua 4:6, he writes, "are the starting point for the literary, *canonical* process, as well as for the *educational* process." This "manifest concern for the educational process," he says, may be regarded as "the taproot of the completed form of the Torah."

## 7. NEW MODES OF HUMAN FATHERING (NEW TESTAMENT)

1. For the evidence of this, see John W. Miller, *The Origins of the Bible, Rethinking Canon History* (New York: Paulist Press, 1994), pp. 6f.

2. Regarding this point, see Jacob Neusner, *Self-Fulfilling Prophecy, Exile and Return in the History of Judaism* (Boston: Beacon Press, 1967), p. 68,

who writes that "much of the law of the Mishnah derived from the age before the document was completed."

3. Hans-Ruedi Weber, *Jesus and the Children: Biblical Resources for Study and Preaching* (Geneva: World Council of Churches, 1979), p. 40.

4. Regarding this, see Shoshana Matzner-Bekerman, *The Jewish Child: Halakhic Perspectives* (New York: KTAV Publishing House, 1984), pp. 227f.

5. An adequate treatment of the father-role as reflected in New Testament scripture still remains to be written. A beginning on this subject has been made by Levi B. Sommers, in his unpublished dissertation for the Faculty of the School of Theology, Fuller Theological Seminary, *Biblical Perspectives on the Role of the Father* (1980).

6. For an analysis of Jesus' teachings on this subject and their continuing relevance, see my *A Christian Approach to Sexuality* (Scottdale: The Mennonite Publishing House, 1971).

7. Hans-Ruedi Weber, *Jesus and the Children.*

8. For a careful analysis of the important issue of Jesus' attitude toward the Torah see John Bowker, *Jesus and the Pharisees* (Cambridge University Press, 1973), pp. 42–52.

9. On Jesus' unique way of addressing God, and how it compared to the traditions of his time, see Geza Vermes, *Jesus and the World of Judaism* (Philadelphia: Fortress Press, 1983), pp. 39, 42.

10. Marcus Borg, Conflict, *Holiness and Politics in the Teaching of Jesus* (Lewistown, N.Y.: Edwin Mellen, 1984), pp. 123–134.

11. For an elaboration of this hypothesis and its implications for our under-standing of Jesus, see my *Jesus at Thirty, A Psychological and Historical Portrait* (Minneapolis: Fortress Press, 1997).

12. This in fact is how these traditions *are* now being interpreted by Carolyn Osiek and David L. Balch, *Families in the New Testament World, Households and House Churches* (Louisville: Westminster John Knox Press, 1997), who draw the conclusion (from their study of New Testament sources) that "The Synoptic Gospels yield a pattern of deep suspicion about families and blood ties" (p. 218).

13. The argument of Osiek and Balch, *Families in the New Testament World,* that these texts are reflective of a post-Pauline shift in Christian ethics toward an "Aristotelian imperative that wives, children, and slaves must be subordinate to the male head of the household" (p. 220) does not sufficiently attend to their stress on husbands *loving* their wives in the same self-giving manner that Christ loved the church. In my opinion these teachings echo Jewish values regarding

the centrality of the father's role in the family and, if anything, voice a critique of the harsh, domineering patriarchalism of Greco-Roman culture.

14. Regarding this, see Robert Hammerton-Kelly, *God the Father, Theology and Patriarchy in the Teaching of Jesus* (Philadelphia: Fortress, 1979), who summarizes (p. 88): "God the Father…was the living reality of early Christian experience, the appellation by which that experience was focused and celebrated in public worship and private prayer."

15. In a remarkable piece of exegetical detective work, Hans-Ruedi Weber, *Jesus and the Children*, pp. 43–51, shows how the early church tended to spiritualize even the few words of Jesus on the subject of "the child," being "more interested in what a child symbolizes than in Jesus' attitude to actual children. This is even more true," he writes, "for the remainder of the New Testament" (p. 49)

16. In an aside, to explain why he was not wanting to be supported by his Corinthian "children," Paul states that children should not have to support their parents, but parents their children (2 Cor 12:14). It is also stated elsewhere that elders must be model fathers who elicit obedience from their children (1 Tm 3:4, 12; Ti 1:6).

17. It is Barclay, *Train Up a Child*, pp. 234–238, who called this to my attention. Not only, he writes, does the New Testament itself have "practically nothing to say about the training of the child" (p. 235), but neither did the early church for the first four centuries. "She provided careful and detailed instruction for her catechumens, and for her ministry, but for her children she provided none at all" (p. 238).

18. According to Talmudic teaching, quoted by Shoshana Matzner-Bekerman, *The Jewish Child*, p. 44, "The covenant of circumcision is considered as important as all the *mitzvot* [commandments] in the Torah together." This practice alone explains "the reason for the survival of the Jews throughout their traumatic history." "Time and Byzantium will become a memory, but the nation which practices circumcision will endure forever."

## 8. The Contemporary Fathering Crisis

1. David Bakan, "Paternity in the Judeo-Christian Tradition," in Allan W. Eister, ed., *Changing Perspectives in the Scientific Study of Religion* (New York: J. Wiley, 1974), p. 204.

2. See Mircea Eliade, *A History of Religious Ideas*, Vol. 1, *From the Stone*

*Age to the Eleusinian Mysteries* (Chicago: University of Chicago Press, 1978), pp. 20–22, 40–44.

3. *Ibid.*, p. 40.

4. On this point and its importance for the development of the family, see David Bakan, *And They Took Themselves Wives: The Emergence of Patriarchy in Western Civilization* (San Francisco: Harper & Row, 1979), p. 27; also Chapters 2 and 3 of this volume.

5. See Bronislaw Malinowski, *The Father in Primitive Psychology* (New York: W. W. Norton, 1927).

6. Andrienne Zihlman, "Motherhood in Transition: From Ape to Human," in Warren B. Miller and Lucile F. Newman, eds., *The First Child and Family Formation* (Chapel Hill: Carolina Population Center, The University of North Carolina, 1978), p. 37. The description that follows is based largely on her sketch of chimpanzee society which she believes provides "the most specific beginning for hypothesizing the characteristics of the population immediately preceding the early hominids" (p. 37).

7. *Ibid.*, p. 47.

8. *Ibid.*, p. 48.

9. *Ibid.*

10. On these myths see Erich Neumann, *The Origins and History of Consciousness*, Bollingen Series XII (New York: Pantheon Books, 1954); Joseph Campbell, *The Hero with a Thousand Faces*, Bollingen Series XVII (Princeton, University Press, 1949); S. N. Kramer, *History Begins at Sumer* (Philadelphia: University of Pennsylvania Press, 1956), pp. 224–226; Mircea Eliade, *A History of Religious Ideas*, pp. 284–289.

11. On the male group as "the birthplace" of masculine consciousness, individuality and "the hero," see Erich Neumann, *The Origins and History of Consciousness*, pp. 140–145.

12. The antiquity of these rites is stressed by Eliade, *A History of Religious Ideas*, p. 25; also their association with the era of the "heroes" and the beginning of the monogamous family, *ibid.*, pp. 285f. On their continuing importance in many primitive tribes as a means of bringing to an end the son's bond with his mother, see William N. Stephens, *The Oedipus Complex: Cross-Cultural Evidence* (New York: The Free Press of Glencoe, 1962).

13. I refer again to the discussion of these matters in Part One of this volume.

14. The way the typical Greek father in antiquity neglected his wife and children (and the consequences of this) are fully documented by Philip Slater, *The Glory of Hera: Greek Mythology and the Greek Family* (Boston: Beacon Press,

1968). According to L. Delaporte, *Mesopotamia: The Babylonian and Assyrian Civilization* (London: Alfred A. Knopf, 1925), p. 85, men seem to have frequently divorced their wives and abandoned their children in that region as well. How this affected their role in the family is reflected in the marginal roles fathers play in Mesopotamian myths and legends. The same is true of the fathers of Canaanite and Egyptian myths. On this see J. W. Miller, "God as Father in the Bible and the Father Image in Several Contemporary Ancient Near Eastern Myths: A Comparison," *Studies in Religion/Sciences Religieuses*, 14/3 (Summer 1985), pp. 347–354 (Chapter 4 in this volume). The strengths and weaknesses of the typical Egyptian father are carefully delineated by Jan Assmann, "Das Bild des Vaters in alten Aegypten," in G. Bornkamm, et al., eds., *Das Vaterbild in Mythos and Geschichte* (Stuttgart: Kohlhammer, 1976), pp. 12–49.

15. For Africa, see H. Collomb and S. Valatin, "The Black African Family," in J. Anthony and C. Koupernik, eds., *The Child and His Family* (New York: J. Wiley, 1970), pp. 359–388; for India, see Sudhir Kakar, "Father and Sons: An Indian Experience," in Stanley Cath, et al., eds., *Father and Child: Developmental and Clinical Perspectives* (Boston: Little, Brown, 1982), pp. 417–442; for China, Japan, and other examples, see the summaries in David B. Lynn, *The Father: His Role in Child Development* (Monterey, California: Brooks/Cole Publishing Co., 1974), pp. 33–44.

16. On the forces and influences involved in the formation of this complex body of literature as the normative scriptures of the Israelite people, see John W. Miller, *The Origins of the Bible, Rethinking Canon History* (New York: Paulist Press, 1994).

17. See R. Harris, "Women in the Ancient Near East," in *The Interpreter's Dictionary of the Bible*, Supplementary Volume (Nashville: Abingdon, 1976), pp. 960–963.

18. See n. 14 above, n. 20 below. This point is often overlooked in feminist discussion of "patriarchy" (so-called). For example, Naomi Goldenberg in *Changing of the Gods: Feminism and the End of Traditional Religions* (Boston: Beacon Press, 1979), p. 37, states that "all recorded history has been patriarchal" and therefore only today (in the wake of the feminist movement) are we about to see "what happens when father-gods die for an entire culture...." The truth is that the father-gods were not altogether alive and well even under patriarchy.

19. See N. Sandars, *The Epic of Gilgamesh* (Middlesex: Penguin Books, 1960), for an idiomatic translation and introduction to this story. On its psychological aspects see Thorkild Jacobson, *The Treasures of Darkness: A*

*History of Mesopotamian Religion* (New Haven: Yale University Press, 1976), pp. 218f.

20. The deities vested with ruling the earth in the ancient Near East (except for Israel) were all sons (not fathers): Marduk in Mesopotamia, Baal in Canaan, Horus in Egypt. According to E. O. James, *The Worship of the Sky-God: A Comparative Study in Semitic and Indo-European Religion* (University of London: The Athlone Press, 1963), p. 8, father-deities tend to be *Deus otiosus* and marginal to the cult "everywhere in primitive states of culture both in the present and the past."

21. Samuel Kramer, *History Begins at Sumer* (see n. 10 above), p. 224, characterizes the "Heroic Ages" in Sumer, Greece, India, and northern Europe as "essentially barbaric," dominated as they were by princes with retinues of armed followers prepared to do their bidding without question "no matter how foolhardy and dangerous the undertaking."

22. At the conclusion of his study of Greek civilization, P. Slater, *The Glory of Hera* (see n. 14 above), poses a similar question (see p. 462).

23. The massive data bearing on the representation of God as father in the Bible is reviewed by Robert Hammerton-Kelly, *God the Father: Theology and Patriarchy in the Teaching of Jesus* (Philadelphia: Fortress, 1979). Relevant to this subject are not only those texts where the term father itself is used, but the characterization of God as "God of the fathers" and "father of the gods" through the transfer to him of the name of the Canaanite father-deity "El" (Gn 33:20; Jos 22:22), as well as many El-epithets. See J. J. M. Roberts, "El," in *Interpreter's Dictionary of the Bible*, Supplementary Volume, pp. 255–258. Indeed, many scholars now believe that "Yahweh" (the most often used biblical name for God) may have originated as a cultic epithet for El (Ps 10:12). However, in striking contrast to Canaanite El, Yahweh is "the jealous one," for "a jealous god [el] is he" (Ex 34:14; cf. Ex 20:5; Dt 5:9; 32:16; Jos 23:19; Nm 25:11). This energetic paternal emotion is at the root of the monotheistic focus that sets biblical religion apart from all other religions of the ancient world (Ex 20:3; Dt 5:7). Regarding this see also Walter Eichrodt, *Theology of the Old Testament*, Vol. 1 (Philadelphia: Westminster Press, 1961), p. 210, n. 1; and Erhard S. Gerstenberger, *Yahweh, The Patriarch, Ancient Images of God and Feminist Theology* (Minneapolis: Fortress, 1996), pp. 8f. Recent feminist claims that the biblical God was also thought of as "mother" are based on passages where he is characterized as engaging in mother-like activities or as having mother-like attributes. On these see P. Trible, "God, Nature of, in the OT," in *The Interpreter's Dictionary of the Bible*, Supplementary Volume, pp. 368f; Virginia

R. Mollenkott, *The Divine Feminine: The Biblical Imagery of God as Female* (New York: Crossroad, 1983). However, a father does not become a mother when likened to a mother, any more than he becomes a rock when likened to a rock (Dt 32:18). Against Sallie McFague, *Metaphorical Theology: Models of God in Religious Language* (Philadelphia: Fortress Press, 1982), "father" is not simply one metaphor among others in the Bible; it is the meaning of his *name* (Is 63:16; Mal 2:10); according to Jesus father *is* his name (Lk 11:2; Jn 17:6, 11, 12, 26).

24. The absence of "hero" themes (so prominent elsewhere in the literature of the ancient Near East) in the patriarchal stories in Genesis is noted by Claus Westermann, *The Promises to the Fathers: Studies in Patriarchal Narratives* (Philadelphia: Fortress Press, 1980), p. 35. On the father generally in the Old Testament, see Lothar Perlitt, "Der Vater im alten Testament," in Bornkamm, et al., eds., *Das Vaterbild in Mythos und Geschichte*, pp. 50–101

25. Concerning the relatively "high status" of women in the Old Testament, see John H. Otwell, *And Sarah Laughed: The Status of Women in the Old Testament* (Philadelphia: Westminster Press, 1977); also Hans Walter Wolff, *Anthropology of the Old Testament* (Philadelphia: Fortress Press, 1974), pp. 169–173.

26. Incest (Lv 18:6–18), transvestism (Dt 22:5), adultery (Ex 20:14), homosexuality (Lv 18:6–18), and sodomy (Lv 18:23) are all proscribed in the legal codes. The Israelite attitude toward rape is expressed in Tamar's protest: "Such a thing is not done in Israel" (2 Sam 13:12). On these "disorders of love" (as he refers to them), see again Wolff, *ibid,* pp. 173–176.

27. On the historic importance of this achievement alone, see E. Wellish, *Isaac and Oedipus: A Study in Biblical Psychology of the Sacrifice of Isaac; The Akedah* (London: Routledge & Kegan Paul, 1953).

28. Concerning the way narrative tradition in the Old Testament arose from paternal instruction in the family, see E. S. Gerstenberger and W. Schrage, *Woman and Man* (Nashville: Abingdon, 1980), p. 35.

29. A particularly striking example of the changes in family values that occurred through the witness of Jews and Christians is cited by Carolyn Osiek and David I. Balch, *Families in the New Testament World, Households and House Churches* (Louisville: Westminster John Knox Press, 1997. They write that "Pagan writers were surprised and even offended that Jews raised all their children. Therefore, the change from the pagan to the Christian values with respect to children was dramatic, a contrast of far-reaching significance. From Jews, Christians took over the value that infanticide was murder, and on Feb. 7,

374 C.E., the Christian emperor Valentinian made killing an infant a capital crime. Karl Marx wrote [they add]: 'We can forgive Christians much, for they taught us to love children'" (p. 66).

30. On these developments see Alexander Mitscherlich, *Society without the Father: A Contribution to Social Psychology* (New York: Harcourt, Brace & World, 1963); and John Nash, "The Father in Contemporary Culture and Current Psychological Literature," *Child Development*, 36 (1965), pp. 261–297.

31. According to a Johns Hopkins University survey (reported in an Associated Press release, *Kitchener Waterloo Record*, October 20, 1980), sexual activity among girls, 15–19, increased to 49.8 percent in 1979 (from 30 percent in 1971); among teenaged males (17–21) 70 percent had engaged in sex. When comparing the sexual revolutions of the nineteenth and twentieth centuries, Gertrude Himmelfarb, in her book *The De-Moralization of Society, From Victorian Virtues to Modern Values* (New York: Vintage Books, 1994), comments that "In contemplating the 'sexual anarchy' of the late nineteenth century, one can hardly fail to see in it portents of the 'sexual revolution' of the late twentieth century. There are indeed significant resemblances between that time and ours. But there is also one overriding difference. A century ago the 'advanced' souls were just that, well in advance of the culture, whereas now they pervade the entire culture. This is the significance of our 'sexual revolution': it is a revolution democratized and legitimized" (pp. 217f.).

32. According to government statistics, out-of-wedlock births in the United States increased 50 percent during the decade of the 1970s. In 1979 one in six American babies was born to an unwed mother (55 percent of all African-American babies). At the same time about half of all new marriages are now ending in divorce, with 60 percent of these involving children.

33. According to Benjamin Schlesinger, *One-Parent Families and Their Children in Canadian Society* (The University of Western Ontario, 1979), p. 89, 10 percent of Canadian families are now one-parent families (involving 850,000 children), with 83 percent of these being mother-led (without fathers). The statistics for the United States are: 14 percent one-parent families (involving 11,311,000 children), 84 percent without fathers. George Miller in an article entitled "Children and the Congress: A Time to Speak Out," *The American Psychologist*, 38 (January 1983), p. 75, writes that "by the end of the decade there is projected to be a 14 percent increase in the number of children under 10. Close to half of these children can expect to live with only one parent at some time during their childhood."

34. Judith Herman, *Father-Daughter-Incest* (Cambridge and London: Harvard University Press, 1981), p. 213, writes that "many of the causes that women have supported most passionately in the last century—temperance, animal rescue, the suppression of vice—can best be understood as attempts to get men out of the barroom, the game pit, the whore house, and into the home."

35. It is estimated that in the United States over one-third of all mothers (35 percent) with children under three are now working outside the home, and that by the time these children are six this percentage almost doubles. See Ross D. Parke, *Fathers* (Cambridge: Harvard University Press, 1981), p. 104.

36. James Dobson, a Christian child clinician who heads up one of these movements, writes in his book, *Straight Talk to Men and Their Wives* (Waco, Texas: Word Books, 1980), p. 21, of having received a revelation to the effect that "if America is going to survive the incredible stresses and dangers it now faces, it will be because husbands and fathers again place their families at the highest level on their system of priorities, reserving a portion of their time and energy for leadership within their homes!"

37. John Nash, "The Father in Contemporary Culture" (see n. 30 above), pp. 264–267.

38. For research reviews see Henry Biller, *Paternal Deprivation: Family, School, Sexuality, and Society* (Lexington, Massachusetts: D. C. Heath and Company, 1974); *Fathers and Families, Paternal Factors in Child Development* (Westport: Auburn House, 1993); David B. Lynn, *The Father: His Role in Child Development*; Ross D. Parke, *Fathers*; Stanley Cath, et al., eds., *Father and Child*; Michael E. Lamb, ed, *The Role of the Father in Child Development* (New York: John Wiley & Sons, 1976; third edition, 1997).

39. See Seymour Fisher and Roger Greenberg, *The Scientific Credibility of Freud's Theories and Therapy* (New York: Basic Books, 1977), especially pp. 396–399.

40. For research on mothering, see Rudolph Schaffer, *Mothering* (Cambridge: Harvard University Press, 1977). On "maternal sensitivity" as a centrally important characteristic in fostering and securing healthy infant development, see especially pp. 79–83.

41. See Richard Atkins, "Discovering Daddy: The Mother's Role," in Cath, et al., *Father and Child* (see n. 15), pp. 139–149; Stanley Greenspan, "'The Second Other': The Role of the Father in Early Personality Formation and the Dyadic-Phalic Phase of Development," *ibid.*, pp. 123–138. In "The Paternal Imperative," *American Scholar* (Winter 1998), pp. 118–126, David Gutmann writes that the father "becomes in the proper season what the psychoanalysts

call a 'transitional object'—a kind of psychological halfway house. Standing apart from the mother, the father provides a secure way station on the son's psychological voyage away from her..." (p. 122).

42. See James M. Herzog, "On Father Hunger: The Father's Role in the Modulation of Aggressive Drive and Fantasy," *ibid.*, pp. 163–174.

43. For a review of the research on gender-identity in boys see Phyllis Tyson, "The Role of the Father in Gender Identity, Urethral Eroticism, and Phallic Narcissism," *ibid.*, pp. 175–187; for girls, see Nancy Chodorow, *The Reproduction of Mothering: Psychoanalysis and the Sociology of Gender* (Berkeley: University of California Press, 1978); Biller, *Fathers and Families*, p. 57. Henry Biller's earlier study is also still important: *Father, Child and Sex Role: Paternal Determinants of Personality Development* (Lexington, Massachusetts: Heath Lexington Books, 1971).

44. The research leading to this breakthrough discovery is reviewed by Ethel Person and Lionel Ovesey, "Psychoanalytic Theory of Gender Identity," *Journal of the American Academy of Psychoanalysis*, 11 (1983), pp. 203–225. Also pertinent in this regard is the evidence (reviewed by Biller, *Fathers and Families*, pp. 58f.) of paternal deprivation among transexual boys who feel trapped in a body of the wrong sex.

45. The research results are summarized by Biller as follows: "The close-binding mother-son relationship that sometimes precedes the expression of homosexuality in males frequently takes place in the context of a distant or otherwise inappropriate father-son relationship" (*ibid.* p. 183). Methodological flaws leading to excessive claims for an exclusively genetic or hormonal determinant in the genesis of homosexuality (based on studies of twins, genetic markers or hormone metabolism) are critiqued by Garland E. Allen, "The Double-Edged Sword of Genetic Determinism, Social and Political Agendas in Genetic Studies of Homosexuality, 1940–1994," in *Science and Homosexualities*, ed. Vernon A. Rosario (New York: Routledge, 1997), pp. 242–270. For a more balanced appraisal, see Richard C. Friedman, *Male Homosexuality, A Contemporary Psychoanalytic Perspective* (New Haven: Yale University Press, 1988), especially Chapter 2, "Psychobiological Considerations," pp. 11–32, where Friedman cautiously concludes that "it seems likely that biological parameters do influence the etiology of homosexuality in subgroups of males. But these effects are probably indirect and partial, and intermediate psychobiological mechanisms remain to be fully established" (p. 32). For Friedman's views regarding the latter (psychobiological mechanisms), see the following note.

46. Charles W. Socarides, "Abdicating Fathers, Homosexual Sons: Psychoanalytic Observations on the Contribution of the Father to the Development of Male Homosexuality," *Father and Child* (see n. 15), p. 512. For similar views, see Richard C. Friedman, *Male Homosexuality*, who cites research pointing to childhood gender-disturbance (more specifically, a feminine or unmasculine self-concept during childhood due in part to a disconnect with the father) as "the single most important causal influence" in the emergence of "predominant or exclusive homosexuality in men" (pp. 74, 77). According to Fisher and Greenberg, *The Scientific Credibility of Freud's Theories and Therapy*, there does not appear to be a single even moderately well-controlled study of parental attitudes among male homosexuals that shows that they refer to their fathers positively or affectionately. On the contrary, they write, "With only a few exceptions, the male homosexual declares that father has been a negative influence in his life. He refers to him with such adjectives as cold, unfriendly, punishing, brutal, distant, detached..." (p. 242).

47. James Herzog, "On Father Hunger" (see n. 42).

48. Stanley Greenspan, "The Second Other" (see n. 41)

49. Linda Gunsberg, "Selected Critical Review of Psychological Investigation of the Early Father-Infant Relationship," in Cath, et al., *Father and Child* (see n. 15), p. 76.

50. James Herzog, "On Father Hunger" (see n. 42), p. 76.

51. For a review of the research on boys' developmental journey during these years, see John Ross, "From Mother to Father: The Boy's Search for a Generative Identity and the Oedipal Era," *Father and Child* (see n. 15), pp. 189–203; for the girl, see Lora Tessman, "A Note on the Father's Contribution to the Daughter's Ways of Loving and Working," *ibid.*, pp. 219–238.

52. This research is reviewed and summarized by Fisher and Greenberg, *The Scientific Credibility of Freud's Theories and Therapy* (see n. 39). In their concluding summary they write that "the evidence is quite convincing that what motivates the boy to identify with the father and his masculinity is not fear but rather father's nurturing friendliness. The boy apparently gives up his competitive struggle with the father because his positive, friendly attitude invites one to become like him."

53. On this see especially Marjorie Leonard, "Fathers and Daughters: The Significance of 'Fathering' in the Psychosexual Development of the Girl," *International Journal of Psychoanalysis*, 47 (1966), pp. 325–334.

54. Lora Tessman (see n. 51), p. 231.

55. Antoine Vergote has written in *The Parental Figures and the*

*Representation of God: A Psychological and Cross-Cultural Study* (The Hague, Paris, New York: Mouton Publishers, 1981), p. 193, that for this reason the father ideally represents "prohibitive law" for both sons and daughters, while the mother's authority is ideally "referential" (to the father). If she imposes herself on the child with a direct authority as "judge," this may contradict her availability and produce emotional disturbances. It is striking, Vergote summarizes on p. 189, that "judge" is the only factor that characterizes the mother figure of the schizophrenic, a fact that concurs with the clinical data according to which the father of the schizophrenic does not assume his paternity. On this point, see also Biller, *Fathers and Families*, who cites research showing that many fathers of adult schizophrenics "had severe conflicts with their wives, often undercutting their attempts to set limits for their children and generally showing them little respect " (p. 217).

56. On this point see Theodore Lidz, "The Family as the Developmental Setting," in James Anthony and Cyrille Kompernik, eds., *The Child and His Family* (New York: John Wiley & Sons, 1970), p. 29.

57. On father-roles during latency and adolescence see John Ross, "Mentorship in Middle Childhood," in S. Cath, et al., eds., *Father and Child* (see n. 15), pp. 243–252; Charles Sarnoff, "The Father's Role in Latency," ibid., pp. 265–274.

58. Calvin Colarusso and Robert Nemiroff, "The Father in Midlife Crisis and the Growth of Paternal Identity," *ibid.*, pp. 315–327.

59. Antoine Vergote, *The Religious Man: A Psychological Study of Religious Attitudes* (Dublin: Gill and Macmillan, 1969), p. 179.

60. Edward Stein, "Fathering: Fact or Fable?" in E. Stein, ed., *Fathering: Fact or Fable?* (Nashville: Abingdon, 1977), p. 11. The research indicating that fathers play an important role in determining children's moral development is reviewed by Esther Blank Greif, "Fathers, Children, and Moral Development," in Lamb, ed., *The Role of the Father in Child Development* (1976; see note 38), pp. 219–236.

61. On this ambivalence and the way it has been variously interpreted from culture to culture see D. A. Köberle, "Vatergott, Väterlichkeit and Vaterkomplex im christlichen Glauben," in Wilhelm Bitter, ed., *Vorträge über das Vaterproblem in Psychotherapie, Religion und Gesellschaft* (Stuttgart: Hippokrates, 1954), pp. 14–26.

62. Research psychologist Bruce Narramore's comments on spanking in his book *Help! I'm a Parent* (Grand Rapids: Zondervan, 1972), pp. 83–87, are just

one example of the way biblical texts on this subject are being interpreted and appropriated with the help of contemporary psychological insights.

63. Further to this point see J. W. Miller, "In Defense of Monotheistic Fathering Religion," *Journal of Religion and Health*, 21 (1982), pp. 62–67 (Chapter 9 in this volume); also Antoine Vergote, *The Religious Man* (see n. 59), pp. 167–197).

## 9. IN DEFENSE OF MONOTHEISTIC FATHER RELIGION

1. On the patriarchal focus of both Jesus himself and canonical Christianity, see Robert Hamerton-Kelly, *God the Father: Theology and Patriarchy in the Teaching of Jesus* (Philadelphia: Fortress Press, 1979), pp. 52–99.

2. For an astute bibliographical survey and analysis of the discussion of these issues, see Carol P. Christ, "The New Feminist Theology: A Review of the Literature," *Religious Studies Review*, 3 (1977), pp. 203–212.

3. Concerning the current scientific status of psychoanalytic thought, see especially S. Fisher and R. Greenberg, *The Scientific Credibility of Freud's Theories and Therapy* (New York: Basic Books, 1977).

4. Verification of the importance of the son's identification with the father for sexual identity and adult heterosexuality is extensive, even though Freud's understanding of *how* this identification comes about has been shown to be in error at points. Again, see Fisher and Greenberg, *Scientific Credibility*, pp. 170–254.

5. On this critical but often neglected point, see M. Leonard, "Fathers and Daughters: The Significance of 'Fathering' in the Psychosexual Development of the Girl," *International Journal of Psychoanalysis*, 47 (1966), pp. 325–334. In her summary Leonard writes that "following the oedipal conflict, the girl must establish a desexualized object-relationship to her father, enabling her later to accept the feminine role without guilt or anxiety and to give love to a young man in her peer group" (p. 332).

6. This would appear to be Carol Christ's conclusion as well. In criticism of Mary Daly's *Beyond God the Father* (Boston: Beacon Press, 1973), she writes ("The New Feminist Theology," p. 206) that "feminists are not likely to be satisfied with Daly's symbols of 'androgynous' humanity and God as the 'Verb.' A premature envisioning of an androgynous future will not assist the new becoming of women."

7. Son or daughter deities either mediate to the parents or displace them. If they displace them, they become the agents of growth-inhibiting neurosis. This,

of course, was a burning issue for early Christianity in its christological contro-versies. On the psychological dynamics involved, see T. Reik, *Dogma and Compulsion: Psychoanalytic Studies of Religion and Myths* (New York: International Universities Press, 1951), pp. 24–161.

8. Concerning the overwhelming power of the incestuous tie, for men espe-cially, and the way religious and social forces may compound it, see especially E. Fromm, *The Heart of Man* (New York: Harper & Row, 1964), pp. 95–150, and *The Anatomy of Human Destructiveness* (Greenwich, Conn.: Fawcett Publications, 1973), pp. 300–481.

9. Many feminist writers, without explaining why, seem to concur. Patricia Doyle, for example, in an essay on "Women and Religion: Psychological and Cultural Implications," in R. Ruether, ed., *Religion and Sexism: Images of Women in the Jewish and Christian Tradition* (New York: Simon & Schuster, 1974), p. 32, writes that "in an ecologically sensitive age, Mariology as well as Mother Earth religion may be appealing, and worthy of resuscitation. I expect, however, that many (and not just feminists) would find exclusive association of divinity with motherhood as confining and tyrannical as the father image many now try to escape, so that the task is to find imagery that transcends sex-specific capacities and awareness."

10. The outstanding exception to this criticism is Nancy Chodorow's *The Reproduction of Mothering: Psychoanalysis and the Sociology of Gender* (Berkeley: University of California Press, 1978), where she argues eloquently that the father's role is essential to the well-being of *both* sexes and that, there-fore, he should play a much larger role than is currently customary in *primary* parenting.

11. On this point Marjorie Leonard, "Fathers and Daughters," p. 332, com-ments as follows: "…when the daughter reaches the phase in her development when she is searching for a love-object, the ability of the father to respond to her needs depends on the extent to which his own oedipal conflict is resolved. He cannot give her desexualized affection if his counter-oedipal response provokes inappropriate defense measures which will then be reciprocated in his daugh-ter's response. Thus, neurosis in the parent is perpetuated in the child."

12. Freud thought that fear of loss of love and disappointment of oedipal wishes provided the chief motivation for the termination of this tie to the father in girls; but because such motives do not have the strength of castration fear in men in their relation to the father, the overcoming of the oedipus complex is much more problematical and incomplete in many women. Freud wrote, "Girls remain in it for an indeterminate length of time; they demolish it late and, even

so, incompletely." *New Introductory Lectures on Psychoanalysis*, Vol. 2 (New York: Penguin Books, 1973), p. 163. On this important issue see also V. Machtlinger, "Psychoanalytic Theory: Preoedipal and Oedipal Phases with Special Reference to the Father," in M. Lamb, ed., *The Role of the Father in Child Development* (New York: John Wiley and Sons, 1976), pp. 277–305.

13. Christ, "The New Feminist Theology," p. 211, seems to be saying something similar when she writes of her discovery that "the experience of motherhood, properly approached, can function for women in ways analogous to the mystic's dark night of the soul, as a time of purgation and integration which opens the self to spiritual experience." Maybe this is the intuition that informs that rather quaint early Christian insight that women "will be saved by childbearing..." (1 Tm 2:15).

14. For elaboration and confirmation of this point I refer again to the writings of Erich Fromm, especially his discussion of "Malignant Aggression" in *The Anatomy of Human Destructiveness*, pp. 300–481; and also, now, the powerful essay by David Gutmann, "The Paternal Imperative," *American Scholar* (Winter 1998), pp. 118–126, where he writes as follows: "Here then is a central paradox of masculine development: The psycho-umbilical ('Golden Cord') tie to the mother is crucial at the beginning of life, but it must, at some critical point, be severed. The boy who persists beyond the proper season as a mother's son will be psychologically vulnerable to the otherwise routine separations inherent in living: in youth, he is at risk to become an addicted delinquent; in adulthood he will probably be an envious brother rather than a good enough father to his own children, while his wife or successive wives will be drained by his chronic neediness and in peril from his violent rages towards women. In later life—if he makes it that far—he may well be a depressed psychosomatic cripple and a drain on the health system" (p. 120).

15. Admittedly the roles prescribed for women in the New Testament are viewed there as the result of a certain characterological inferiority on their part ("she is to keep silent, for Adam was formed first, then Eve; and Adam was not deceived, but the woman was deceived and became a transgressor" (1 Tm 2:12–14). A developmental psychoanalytic perspective opens the door for a more positive interpretation of the feminine role in a patriarchal society.

10. THE REFUTATION OF THE "FATHER" IN GOD IN FEMINIST
    THEOLOGIES

1. Friedrich Nietzsche, *Beyond Good and Evil, Prelude to a Philosophy of the Future*, Translated with commentary by Walter Kaufmann (New York: Vintage Books, 1966), p. 66.

2. *Ibid.*, p. 203.

3. I am not meaning to imply that this was the only factor in the rise of Nazism. That disorders in fathering *were* a factor is the conclusion also drawn by Peter Loewenberg, "The Pschohistorical Origins of the Nazi Youth Cohort," in *Decoding the Past: The Psychohistorical Approach* (New York: Alfred Knopf, 1983), pp. 240–283.

4. Rosemary Radford Ruether, *Sexism and God-Talk, Toward a Feminist Theology* (Boston: Beacon Press, 1983), p. 1. For an analysis and overview of these religious trends, see Francis Martin, *The Feminist Question, Feminist Theology in the Light of Christian Tradition* (Grand Rapids: Eerdmans, 1994), especially Ch. 5, "An Historical Overview of Feminism and Feminist Theology," pp. 145–167.

5. Elisabeth Schüssler Fiorenza, *Sharing Her Word, Feminist Biblical Interpretation in Context* (Boston: Beacon Press, 1998), p. 149.

6. The complexities and uncertainties involved in this search for alternatives are exemplified in the works of Naomi R. Goldenberg, *Changing of the Gods, Feminism and the End of Traditional Religions* (Boston: Beacon Press, 1979); *The End of God, Important Directions for a Feminist Critique of Religion in the Works of Sigmund Freud and Carl Jung* (Ottawa: University of Ottawa Press, 1981), and Carol Ochs, *Behind the Sex of God, Toward a New Consciousness—Transcending Matriarchy and Patriarchy* (Boston: Beacon Press, 1977). Ochs is persuaded that "matriarchy and patriarchy are two fundamental and opposing ways of life in this world and of understanding reality" (p. 110), neither of which is viable. Her alternative is a form of degendered pantheism. The alternative Goldenberg leans toward is what she calls "the imaginal products of women" reflected on in a manner which might be called religious.

7. Goldenberg, *Changing of the Gods*, p. 37.

8. *Ibid.*, p. 72. "When a symbol as pervasive as that of the father-god begins to die," Goldenberg writes, "tremendous anxiety is generated. Other images arise to take its place almost immediately. Candidates for different god images are already being nominated either to replace the father-god or to provide him

with a female retinue. A survey of these new images shows that some are more conducive to freedom of thought than others."

9. *Ibid.*, p. 140. Elsewhere Goldenberg states that "It seems highly likely that the West is on the brink of developing a new mysticism—post-Christian, post-Judaic. It will most probably be a type of mysticism which emphasizes the *continual observation of psychic imagery*" (p. 120). In this new pantheon of gods, she states, the father-god will be among them, but no longer will "Christ and Yahweh…behave as egotistical, spoiled children in our psyches—they will no longer keep us from giving our attention to other members of our psychic families" (p. 83).

10. Rosemary Radford Ruether, *Women and Redemption, A Theological History* (Minneapolis: Fortress Press, 1998), pp. 280f.)

11. Schüssler Fiorenza, *Sharing Her Word*, p. 178.

12. On this development see the essays in *Horizons in Feminist Theology, Identity, Tradition, and Norms*, Rebecca S. Chopp and Sheila Greeve Davaney, eds. (Minneapolis: Fortress Press, 1997). For examples of the impact these developments are having on biblical studies, see Patrick D. Miller, "Imagining God," in *Women, Gender, and Christian Community*, Jane Dempsey Douglass and James F. Kay, eds. (Louisville: Westminster John Knox Press, 1997), pp. 3–12; Erhard S. Gerstenberger, *Yahweh, The Patriarch, Ancient Images of God and Feminist Theology* (Minneapolis: Fortress Press, 1996).

13. Rosemary Radford Ruether, "Patriarchy," in *Dictionary of Feminist Theologies*, Letty M. Russel and J. Shannon Clarkson, eds. (Louisville: Westminster John Knox Press, 1996), p. 205.

14. Reuther, *Sexism and God-Talk*, p. 113.

15. *Ibid.*, p. 111.

16. Schüssler Fiorenza, *Sharing Her Word*, p. 179.

17. Sandra Lipsitz Bem, *The Lenses of Gender, Transforming the Debate on Sexual Inequality* (New Haven: Yale University Press, 1993), p. 192. These views are also more or less endorsed by Deborah L. Rhode, *Speaking of Sex, The Denial of Gender Inequality* (Cambridge: Harvard University Press, 1997), who states "that as long as sex-linked traits remain, the pressures for conformity will limit individual choice" (p. 239).

18. *Ibid.*, pp. 186f.

19. Bem adds that "Full-time parenting when children are young should be regarded as much the same kind of personal career sacrifice for the good of the society as serving in the armed forces—in which case the women who do so should be paid for their effort and should also be helped in their transition

into the 'civilian' economy with some kind of analogue to the GI bill" (*Ibid.*, p. 187).

20. Janet Z. Giele, "Decline of the Family: Conservative, Liberal, and Feminist Views," in *Promises to Keep, Decline and Renewal of Marriage in America*, David Popenoe, Jean Bethke Elshtain, and David Blankenhorn, eds. (Lanham: Rowman & Littlefield, 1996), p. 101. On the impact of these views on contemporary social work theory and practice, see Janet A. Nes and Peter Iadicola, "Toward a Definition of Feminist Social Work: A comparison of Liberal, Radical, and Socialist Models," *Social Work* (January 1989), pp. 12–21. For similar points of view among feminist theologians, see the articles on "Family" and "Mother/Motherhood," by Lee McGee and Nancy J. Duff, in *Dictionary of Feminist Theologies*, Letty M. Russell and J. Shannon Clarkson, eds. (Louisville: Westminster John Knox Press, 1996), pp. 98, 187. The pervasive influence of these views on teaching about marriage in recently published undergraduate marriage and family textbooks is documented by Norval Glenn, *Closed Hearts, Closed Minds, The Textbook Story of Marriage, A Report to the Nation from the Council on Families* (New York: Institute for American Values, 1997).

21. Plato, *The Republic*, translated with an introduction by Desmond Lee, Second Edition, Revised (London: Penguin Books, 1988), Part VI: Women and the Family, pp. 449–470. For a discussion of Plato's feminism in this section, see Nickolas Pappas, *Routledge Philosophy Guide Book to Plato and the Republic* (London and New York: Routledge, 1995), pp. 104–110.

22. Margaret Mead, *Male and Female, A Study of the Sexes in a Changing World* (New York: William Morrow & Company, 1949), is less sanguine. In a remarkable chapter entitled, "Human Fatherhood is a Social Invention," she argues that the continued existence of the family as a patterned arrangement of the two sexes in which men play a role in the nurturing of children, even though a primary condition of humanity, cannot be taken for granted, since large scale abrogations of such family structures have already occurred—not among simple savages, she notes, living close to the subsistence edge, but among great nations and strong empires (and she cites several examples from ancient Peru, nineteenth century Russia, Nazi Germany). "So far," she warns, "no break in the family pattern has been prolonged enough to eradicate men's memories of how valuable it was." Still, she adds, "this continuance of the two-parent family to date, its re-establishment after catastrophic or ideological destruction, is not…any guarantee that this will always be the case, [or]…this will always be so" (pp. 194f.).

23. Phyllis A. Bird, *Feminism and the Bible, A Critical and Constructive Encounter* (Winnipeg: Canadian Mennonite Bible College, 1994), p. 40. For many feminists, Bird writes, the Bible is irrelevant, but still engages them as "a sign of patriarchal bondage to which...they cannot and will not return."

24. Ted Peters, *God—The World's Future, Systematic Theology for a Postmodern Era* (Minneapolis: Fortress Press, 1992), p. 114.

25. On the impact of feminist theologies of this type, see especially Elizabeth Achtemeir, "Exchanging God for 'No Gods': A Discussion of Female Language for God," in *Speaking the Christian God, The Holy Trinity and the Challenge of Feminism*, Alvin F. Kimel, Jr., ed. (Grand Rapids: Eerdmans, 1992), pp. 1–16, who writes that "No aspect of the feminist movement has affected the church's life more basically than has that movement's attempts to change the language used in speaking to or about God" (p. 1).

26. Peters, *God—the World's Future*, p. 114.

27. *Ibid.*

28. This point is acknowledged by virtually everyone who writes on this subject, whatever his or her perspective. See, for example, the essay by Thomas F. Torrance, "The Christian Apprehension of God the Father," in *Speaking the Christian God, The Holy Trinity and the Challenge of Feminism*, Alvin F. Kimel, Jr., ed. (Grand Rapids: William B. Eerdmans, 1992), pp. 120–143.

29. The Bible is quite candid about Israel's long, hard and, at first, unsuccessful struggle with alternative gods and religions (see the accounts in Joshua, Judges, Samuel, Kings, Ezra, Nehemiah). Only through several major reforms (those of Hezekiah and Josiah during the kingship period, and those of Ezra and Nehemiah during the period of Israel's restoration) was the worship of Yahweh alone established as the faith of the Israelite people as a whole. Regarding this struggle and these reforms and their bearing on the formation of the Bible, see John W. Miller, *The Origins of the Bible, Rethinking Canon History* (New York: Paulist Press, 1994).

30. On the nature and uniqueness of this ascription, see John W. Miller, "God as Father in the Bible and the Father Image in Several Contemporary Ancient Near East Myths: A Comparison," *Studies in Religion* 14/3 (1985), pp. 347–354 (Chapter 4 in this volume); also Frank Moore Cross, *Canaanite Myth and Hebrew Epic, Essays in the History of the Religion of Israel* (Cambridge: Harvard University Press, 1973), pp. 42–47.

31. The father language for God in both Testaments has been reviewed many times, most recently by Francis Martin, *The Feminist Question*, pp. 265–292.

32. Yahweh is pictured occasionally as acting with a tenderness and care that is mother-like (Is 42:14; 45:10; 49:15; 66:13), but nowhere in either Testament is he ever *addressed* as mother or said to be mother. On these linguistic distinctions (between simile and metaphor) and their importance, see Roland M. Frye, "Language for God and Feminist Language: Problems and Principles," in *Speaking the Christian God*, pp. 17–43. Frye characterizes the symbol "father" for God as a "structural metaphor" underlying "the entire organism of belief...to which different parts of the living body of faith connect and through which they function" (p. 42). On these issues, see also John W. Miller, "Depatriarchalizing God in Biblical Interpretation: A Critique," *Catholic Biblical Quarterly* 48 (1986), pp. 609–16 (Chapter 5 in this volume).

33. What is now happening in this regard in America is the theme of a growing body of literature, summarized by David Blankenhorn, *Fatherless America, Confronting Our Most Urgent Social Problem* (Basic Books, 1995), especially Chapter 2, "Fatherless Society," pp. 25–48. For the statistics, see Wade F. Horn, *Father Facts*, third edition (National Fatherhood Initiative, 600 Eden Road, Building E, Lancaster, PA 17601).

34. This is the way fatherhood is defined in *Dictionary of Feminist Theologies*, p. 205. This recently published dictionary has no article on "Fathers/Fatherhood" corresponding to its article on "Mothers/Motherhood." In an article on "Patriarchy" we read of "rule of the father" and "male heads of families over dependent persons in the household" (p. 205).

35. Peter J. Wilson, *Man, The Promising Primate, The Conditions of Human Evolution, Second Edition* (New Haven and London: Yale University Press, 1983), p. 59.

36. Wilson, *ibid.*, p. 95. For a comparable account and similar conclusions regarding fatherhood as the transitional event in the emergence of "humanity," see Margaret Mead, *Male and Female*, pp. 183–200.

37. Nancy J. Duff, "Mothers/Motherhood," *Dictionary of Feminist Theologies*, p. 187.

38. *Ibid.* For essays acknowledging, assessing and calling into question this neglect of children's needs in feminist thought, see *Religion, Feminism, & the Family*, Anne Carr and Mary Stewart Van Leeuwen, eds. (Louisville: Westminster John Knox Press, 1996), especially the essay by Mary Stewart Van Leeuwen, "Re-Inventing the Ties That Bind, Feminism and the Family at the Close of the Twentieth Century," pp. 33–52, in which insights from development psychology are used to show the detrimental effects of father-absence on children of both sexes.

39. Hans Sebold, *Momism: The Silent Disease of America* (Chicago: Nelson Hall, 1976).

40. On this, see Rudolf Schaffer, *Mothering* (Cambridge: Harvard University Press, 1977).

41. On the father's critically important role, even during this first year of a child's life, see Richard Atkins, "Discovering Daddy: The Mother's Role," in Stanley Cath, et al., eds., *Father and Child: Developmental and Clinical Perspectives* (Boston: Little, Brown, 1982), pp. 139–149; Stanley Greenspan, "'The Second Other'": The Role of the Father in Early Personality Formation and the Dyadic-Phallic Phase of Development," *ibid.*, pp. 123–138.

42. The research leading to this breakthrough discovery is reviewed by Ethel Person and Lionel Oversey, "Psychoanalytic Theories of Gender Identity," *Journal of the American Academy of Psychoanalysis*, 11 (1983), pp. 203–225.

43. So urgent is a child's own felt need for a father during the second year of his life that one researcher, James M. Herzog, has termed it "father hunger" ("On Father Hunger: The Father's Role in the Modulation of Aggressive Drive and Fantasy," *Father and Child*, pp. 163–174), and another likens the father in his role at this time of his children's lives to that of a lifeguard rescuing a child desperately trying to reach shore while being pursued by a dragon (Stanley Greenspan, "'The Second Other,'" *Ibid.*, pp. 123–138).

44. Regarding this, see Seymour Fischer and Roger Greenberg, *The Scientific Credibility of Freud's Theories and Therapy* (New York: Basic Books, 1977), especially pp. 396–399.

45. For a discussion of these issues from the perspective of developmental psychoanalysis, see John W. Miller, "The Contemporary Fathering Crisis: The Bible and Research Psychology," *The Conrad Grebel Review*, Fall (1983), pp. 21–37 (Chapter 8 in this volume); "In Defense of Monotheistic Father Religion," *Journal of Religion and Health*, 21/1 (1982), pp. 62–67 (Chapter 9 in this volume). For a recent summation of evidence of the ways in which children suffer when fathers are absent, see Norman Dennis and George Erdos, *Families Without Fatherhood*, Second Edition, The IEA Health and Welfare Unit, Choice in Welfare No. 12 (London: IEA Health and Welfare Unit, 1993).

46. Rita M. Gross *Feminism & Religion, An Introduction* (Boston: Beacon Press, 1996), p. 163.

47. *Ibid.*, p. 164.

48. Gerda Lerner, *The Creation of Patriarchy* (New York: Oxford University Press, 1986).

49. *Ibid.*, p. 229. This issue remains unaddressed in her sequel volume, *The*

*Creation of Feminist Consciousness, From the Middle Ages to Eighteen-Seventy* (New York: Oxford, 1993).

50. Don Browning, "Biology, Ethics, and Narrative in Christian Family Theory," in *Promises to Keep, Decline and Renewal of Marriage in America*, David Popenoe, Jean Bethke Elshtain and David Blankenhorn, eds. (Lanham: Rowman & Littlefield Publishers, 1996), pp. 121–123.

51. See Adrienne Zihlman, "Motherhood in Transition: From Ape to Human," in Warren B. Miller and Lucile F. Newman, eds., *The First Child and Family Formation* (Chapel Hill: Carolina Population Center, The University of North Carolina, 1978), for a description of chimpanzee society which, she believes, provides "the most specific beginning for hypothesizing the characteristics of the population immediately preceding the early hominids" (p. 37). For a summary of the evidence bearing on fathering among the prehominid primates, see also Wilson, *Man the Promising Primate*, who states that "on the whole it can be said that most primate males are unable to identify their children" (p. 48).

52. For details, see Helen E. Fisher, *The Sex Contract, The Evolution of Human Behavior* (New York: Quill, 1982), and my essay, "Origins of the Father-Involved Family" (Chapter 2 in this volume).

53. See Fisher, *The Sex Contract*, pp. 119–122.

54. Marija Gimbutas, *The Civilization of the Goddess*, Joan Marler, ed. (HarperSanFrancisco, 1991), especially p. 349. The period surveyed is "Old European society" from about 5500 to 3500 B.C.E.

55. *Ibid.*, p. 223.

56. Bronislaw Malinowski, *The Father in Primitive Psychology* (New York: W. W. Norton, 1927).

57. On the importance of culture in overcoming what he calls "the male problematic" and creating the father-involved family, see again Browning, "Biology, Ethics, and Narrative," p. 123. "According to evolutionary ecologists," he states, "paternal certainty is a necessary, but not sufficient, condition for the development of paternal investment" (p. 123).

58. On this development see my essay, "Male-Centered Reproductive Biology and the Dynamics of Biblical Patriarchy" (Chapter 3 in this volume).

59. For Egyptian tradition in this regard, see "The Instruction of the Vizier Ptah-hotep," an instructional text from the third millennium (2450 B.C.E.), in *Ancient Near Eastern Texts*, James B. Pritchard, ed. (Princeton: Princeton University Press, 1950), p. 413 (lines 200–209 and 330–339); the most extensive collection of Mesopotamian tradition in this regard are the sixty-seven

family laws (case laws 128–195) at the heart of "The Code of Hammurabi," dating from the first half of the second millennium (*Ibid.*, pp. 171–175). This remarkable collection begins with the decree: "If a seignior acquired a wife, but did not draw up the contracts for her, that woman is no wife."

60. Regarding this aspect of the Bible's teachings, see David Mace, *Hebrew Marriage: A Sociological Study* (London: The Epworth Press, 1953), and the essays in the previous sections of this volume. On the formation and role of the Hebrew scriptures, see again my *Origins of the Bible.*

61. Ernst Troeltsch, *The Social Teaching of the Christian Churches*, Vol. 1 (New York: The Macmillan Company, 1931), p. 287. On these developments, see also David Bakan, *And They Took Themselves Wives: The Emergence of Patriarchy in Western Civilization* (San Francisco: Harper & Row, 1979).

62. John Paul II, *Crossing the Threshold of Hope* (Toronto: Alfred A. Knopf, 1994), p. 228.


## 11. WHICH WAY AHEAD?

1. John Locke, "An Essay Concerning the True Original Extent and End of Civil Government," in *Great Books of the Western World*, Robert Maynard Hutchins, ed. (Chicago: Encyclopedia Britannica, 1952), p. 36.

2. *Ibid.*, p. 38.

3. David Bakan, *And They Took Themselves Wives: The Emergence of Patriarchy in Western Civilization* (San Francisco: Harper & Row, 1979), p. 174; see also Jay Fliegelman, *Prodigals and Pilgrims: The American Revolution Against Patriarchal Authority, 1750–1800* (Cambridge: Cambridge University Press, 1982), p. 4.

4. I fear the call for a new marital ethic of "equal regard" in *From Culture Wars to Common Ground, Religion and the American Family Debate*, eds. Don S. Browning and Ian S. Evison (Louisville: Westminster John Knox Press, 1997), pp. 244–246, may turn out to be more symptomatic than remedial of the crisis in family values we are facing. The language itself ("equal regard") obscures the diversity of roles and challenges men and women must take on when becoming marital partners and parents. Further to this issue see John W. Miller, "A Response to Don Browning's 'Christian Equal Regard and the Male Problematic,'" in *Equal Regard and Its Critics*, eds. Don S. Browning and David Blankenhorn, forthcoming from the Institute for American Values (1841 Broadway, Suite 211, New York, New York 10023).

5. Diane Tennis, *Is God the Only Reliable Father?* (Philadelphia:

Westminster, 1985), p. 9. For compelling evidence of the way feminizing God intersects with and reinforces "father-ineffective" family structure, see Michael Carrol, *The Cult of the Virgin Mary: Psychological Origins* (Princeton: Princeton University Press, 1986).

6. *Ibid.*, p. 114.

7. Theodore Stoneberg, "The Tasks of Men in Families," *The Family Handbook*, Herbert Anderson, Don S. Browning, Ian S. Evison and Mary Stewart Van Leeuwen, eds. (Louisville: Westminster John Knox, 1998), p. 71.

8. William Johnson Everett, *Blessed Be the Bond: Christian Perspectives on Marriage and Family* (Philadelphia: Fortress, 1985), pp. 126f.

9. Hans Sebold, *Momism: The Silent Disease of America* (Chicago: Nelson Hall, 1976), pp. 81–83.

10. Anita Spencer, *Mothers Are People Too: A Contemporary Analysis of Motherhood* (New York/Ramsey: Paulist Press, 1984), pp. 60–65.

11. For an excellent study resource, see also Gordon MacDonald, *The Effective Father* (Wheaton: Tyndale House, 1977). MacDonald identifies six principles for effective fathering, the first being the simple recognition that this is "one of my life's highest priorities...."

12. Samuel Osherson, *Finding Our Fathers: The Unfinished Business of Manhood* (New York: The Free Press, 1986), p. 4.

13. Allan Bloom, *The Closing of the American Mind* (New York: Simon & Schuster, 1987), p. 105.

14. For a sobering analysis of the way father-deprivation in Germany brought about by World War I contributed to the formation of the Nazi Youth Cohorts which became the foundation for Hitler's rise to power and the traumatic events leading up to World War II, see Peter Loewenberg, *Decoding the Past: The Psychohistorical Approach* (New York: Alfred Knopf, 1983), pp. 240–283 ("The Psychohistorical Origins of the Nazi Youth Cohort").

## A BIBLICAL CHARTER OF CHILDREN'S RIGHTS (GEN 22)

1. E. A. Speiser, *Genesis*, The Anchor Bible (New York: Doubleday, 1964), p. 164.

2. Erich Wellisch, *Isaac and Oedipus: A Study in Biblical Psychology of the Sacrifice of Isaac: The Akedah* (London: Routledge & Kegan Paul, 1953).

3. *Ibid.*, pp. 98f.

4. *Ibid.*, p. 95.

5. *Ibid.*, p. 93.

6. *Ibid.*, p. 67.

7. In his collection of recorded conversations with contemporary Jewish leaders entitled *The God I Believe In* (New York: The Free Press, 1994), Joshua O. Haberman relates the following anecdote told him by the Jewish philosopher Emil L. Fackenheim. "A Hasid once told me [Fackenheim said] 'I want to see you.' I asked, 'Why?' He said, 'I have something to teach you.' So, he showed up, about twenty-five years old, in his black garb and *payot* [side curls]. What I remember was this question: 'Did it ever occur to you that the God who asks Abraham to do the *akeda* [binding of Isaac as a sacrifice] sends an angel to stop it?' And he said, 'God was fed up with Abraham; when he asked him to sacrifice his son—that was the test—He wanted Abraham to say no!'" Haberman commented, "That's a beautiful lesson." Fackenheim replied: "That's a tremendous thing" (p. 43). For a similar understanding, see Henry Abramovitch, "Images of the 'Father' in Psychology and Religion," Chapter 2, in *The Role of the Father in Child Development*, Michael E. Lamb, ed. (New York: John Wiley & Sons, Third Edition, 1997), who writes: "Having been ready to kill, he [Abraham] looks up and conceives new possibilities and displacements for this bloody urge. This resolution is part of the horrible fascination bound up in the story: the reader must face his own hidden feelings" (p. 27).

## EPILOGUE

1. (Englewood, Colorado: Libraries Unlimited, 1994).

2. (New York and New Jersey: Paulist Press, 1989).

3. Henry B. Biller and Jon Lopez Kimpton, "The Father and the School-Aged Child," in *The Role of the Father in Child Development*, ed. Michael E. Lamb, 3rd ed. (New York: John Wiley, 1997), p. 143.

4. *Fathers* (Cambridge: Harvard University Press, 1981), p. 4.

5. Daniel R. Miller and Guy E. Swanson, *The Changing American Parent* (New York: John Wiley, 1958).

6. Mel Roman and William Haddad, with Susan Manso, *The Disposable Parent: The Case for Joint Custody* (New York: Penguin Books, 1979), p. 85.

7. Michael E. Lamb, "Fathers and Child Development: An Introductory Overview and Guide," *The Role of the Father in Child Development*, ed. Michael E. Lamb, 3rd ed. (New York: John Wiley, 1997), p. 1.

8. *Of Woman Born: Motherhood as Experience and Institution*, Tenth Anniversary Edition (New York: Norton, 1986), p. 57.

9. Miller, *Faith and Fathering*, pp. 5–39.

10. (New York: St. Martin's Press, 1987), p. 187.

11. (London: Achilles Heel, 1983).

12. Hearn, *Birth and Afterbirth*, p. 51.

13. Trans. Alice West, rev. ed. (New York: Penguin Books, 1985).

14. *Male and Female: A Study of the Sexes in a Changing World* (New York: Morrow, 1949).

15. Mead, p. 189.

16. *Manhood in the Making: Cultural Concepts of Masculinity* (New Haven and London: Yale University Press, 1990), pp. 42–48.

17. See, e.g., Mary Daly, *Beyond God the Father* (Boston: Beacon Press, 1973); Mary Daly, *Pure Lust: Elemental Feminist Philosophy* (Boston: Beacon Press, 1984); Mary Daly, with Jane Caputi, *Webster's First New Intergalactic Wickedary of the English Language* (Boston: Beacon Press, 1987); Kate Millett, *Sexual Politics* (New York: Doubleday, 1970); Dale Spender, *Man Made Language* (London: Routledge and Kegan Paul, 1980); Sally Cline and Dale Spender, *Reflecting Men at Twice Their Natural Size* (New York: Henry Holt, 1987); Adrienne Rich, *On Lies, Secrets, and Silence: Selected Prose 1966–1978* (New York: Norton, 1979); and Adrienne Rich, *Of Woman Born: Motherhood as Experience and Institution*, Tenth Anniversary Edition (New York: Norton, 1986).

18. *Of Woman Born*, p. 127.

19. *Refusing to Be a Man: Essays on Sex and Justice* (Portland, Oregon: Breitenbush Books, 1989), reprinted (New York: Penguin USA, Meridian Books, 1990).

20. *Iron John: A Book About Men* (Reading, Massachusetts: Addison-Wesley, 1990).

21. *Where the Two Came to Their Father: A Navaho War Ceremonial Given by Jeff King*, ed. Maud Oakes and Joseph Campbell, 3rd ed. (Princeton: Princeton University Press, 1991).

22. Rev. ed. (New York: Collier, 1962).

23. (New York: Pocket Books, 1993).

24. (New York: Delacorte, 1992).

25. (New York: Random House, 1968).

26. (New York: John Wiley, 1997).

27. See, e.g., Henry B. Biller, *Fathers and Families: Paternal Factors in Child Development* (Westport, CT: Auburn House, 1993); Henry B. Biller and Richard S. Solomon, *Child Maltreatment and Paternal Deprivation: A Manifesto for Research, Prevention, and Treatment* (Lexington, MA: Lexington

Books, 1986); Martin Greenberg, *The Birth of a Father* (New York: Continuum, 1985); Jerrold Lee Shapiro, Michael J. Diamond, and Martin Greenberg, eds., *Becoming a Father: Contemporary, Social, Developmental, and Clinical Perspectives* (New York: Springer, 1995); Michael E. Lamb, ed., *The Role of the Father in Child Development*, 3rd ed. (New York: John Wiley, 1997); James A. Levine, *Who Will Raise the Children? New Options for Fathers (and Mothers)* (Philadelphia and New York: Lippincott, 1976); James A. Levine and Todd L. Pinsky, *Working Fathers: New Strategies for Balancing Work and Family* (Reading, Massachusetts: Addison-Wesley, 1997); Robert A. Lewis and Marvin B. Sussman, eds., *Men's Changing Roles in the Family* (New York: Haworth, 1986); Robert A. Lewis and Robert E. Salt, eds., *Men in Families* (Beverly Hills, CA: Sage, 1986); and Frank A. Pedersen, ed., *The Father-Infant Relationship: Observational Studies in the Family Setting* (New York: Praeger, 1980).

28. *Fathers*, p. 115.

29. *Fatherless America: Confronting Our Most Urgent Social Problem* (New York: Basic Books, 1995).

30. *Male and Female*, p. 193.

# INDEX

Abba, 76, 79
Abraham, 20, 26; child sacrifice, 19, 24, 30, 31, 58, 59, 137–41; circumcision of son, 61
Abuse of children. *See* Child abuse
Abuse of wife. *See* Wife abuse
Adam, 15–16
Adultery, 56
Aeschylus, 20
Aggression, 97
American Men's Studies Association, 145
Anath, 115
Aristotle, 20
Ashteroth, 115

Baal, 36, 38–40, 52, 115
Bakan, David, 22, 23, 43–44, 87, 128
Barclay, William, 65
Benson, Leonard, 149
Bern, Sandra Lipsitz, 112–13
*Beyond Good and Evil* (Nietzsche), 110–11
Bible, 128; and fathering, 91–93, 101, 128; God as father, 41–44, 115–16; and patriarchy, 3, 4, 5; *see also* New Testament
*Biblical Faith and Fathering: Why We Call God "Father"* (Miller), 143–44
Biller, Henry B., 144
Bird, Phyllis, 114
*Birth and Afterbirth: A Materialist Account* (Hearn), 146
Blankenhorn, David, 149–50
Bloom, Allan, 133
Bly, Robert, 148
Borg, Marcus, 76
Browning, Don, 121
Btyk, Felix, 61

Carcopino, Jerome, 66
Castration complex, 99
Cato, 65–66
Celibacy, 81, 94–95
*Changing American Parent, The,* 145
*Changing the Gods, Feminism and the End of Traditional Religions* (Goldenberg), 112

Child abuse, 23–24, 27

Child sacrifice, 19, 27–30;
    Abraham, 19, 24, 30, 31, 58,
    59, 137–41;
    as birth control, 29

*Children Without Men*
    (Ostrovsky), 148

Christianity, 56, 73, 82, 93, 129–
    31; *see also* specific headings,
    e.g.: Bible

Circumcision, 60–62, 70, 81, 82

*Closing of the American Mind,*
    *The* (Bloom), 133

*Code of Hammurabi,* 24, 25, 123

Conception. *See* Reproduction

Corporal punishment, 102

Creation, 15–16

*Creation of Patriarchy, The*
    (Lerner), 20, 121

Cross, Frank Moore, 49, 50

Crossing the Threshold of Hope
    (John Paul II), 124

Developmental psychoanalysis,
    104–09

*Disposable Parent, The* (Roman
    and Haddad), 145

Divorce, 25, 82

Education, 64–69, 70

El, 38–39, 49, 50, 52, 115

Eliade, Mircea, 88

Engels, Friedrich, 147

*Enuma Elis,* 36–38

Everett, William Johnson, 131

Fatherhood: and Bible, 73–82,
    91–93; contemporary crisis,
    94–95; cultural aspects, 4,
    11–17; historical considera-
    tions, 15–16; and Judaism,
    55–70; origins of, 88–93;
    psychological fathering, 13,
    16; *see also* Fathers; and spe-
    cific headings, e.g.:
    Patriarchy; Rituals

*Fatherhood: A Sociological*
    *Perspective* (Benson), 149

*Fatherless America*
    (Blankenhorn), 149–50

*Father Love: What We Need,*
    *What We Seek, What We Must*
    *Create* (Louv), 148

Fathers: and aggression in
    children, 97; castration com-
    plex, 99; and conscience for-
    mation, 96; early involvement
    in children's lives, 101;
    and gender-identity, 97; God
    as father, 5–6, 41–44, 45–52,
    55, 70, 79, 104–09; and
    homosexuality, 97–98; as
    "second others,"47, 97; as
    teachers, 64–69, 80; and vul-
    nerability of children, 26–27;
    *see also* Fatherhood

Feminism, 111–24

*Feminism and Religion* (Gross),
    120–21

Fidelity. *See* Marital fidelity

*Finding Our Fathers: The Unfinished Business of Manhood* (Osherson), 132

Fiorenza, Elisabeth Schüssler. *See* Schüssler Fiorenza, Elisabeth

First born, redemption of, 58–60, 70, 82

Fisher, Helen, 16

Freud, Sigmund, 96, 97, 98–99

Gender equality, 113–14

Gender-identity, 97, 119

*Gender of Oppression: Men, Masculinity, and the Critique of Marxism* (Hearn), 147

Giele, Janet, 113

*Gilgamesh Epic,* 38, 91

Gilmore, David D., 147

Gimbutas, Marija, 122

God: as father, 5–6, 41–44, 45–52, 55, 70, 79, 104–09; as feminine, 3, 5, 46, 48, 49, 51–52; as genderless, 3, 5, 45, 46, 49

Goldenberg, Naomi, 112

Gospels, 73–78

Gross, Rita, 120–21

Haddad, William, 145

*Hammurabi, Code of. See Code of Hammurabi*

Hearn, Jeff, 146

Heterosexuality, 16

Homer, 148

Homosexuality, 97; same-sex marriage, 151

Incest, 56

Infanticide, 27–30

*Iron John* (Bly), 148

Isaac, 20; *see also* Abraham

Isis, 40–41

John Paul II, Pope, 124

*Journal of Men's Studies, The,* 145

Judah, 26

Judaism, 55–70, 71–73, 82, 93, 129

*Kiddushin,* 72, 73

Lamb, Michael E., 149

Latency, 100

Lerner, Gerda, 20, 22–23, 121

Locke, John, 127–28

Louv, Richard, 148

Mace, David, 21–22

*Male and Female* (Mead), 147

Malinowski, Bronislaw, 13, 122–23

*Man, the Promising Primate* (Wilson), 117–18

*Manhood in the Making* (Gilmore), 147

Marital bond, 56, 82, 100; *see also* Sexual bond

Marital fidelity, 26, 30, 31, 56, 78–79

Matriarchy, 122–23
Matzner-Bekerman, Shoshana, 62
Mead, Margaret, 147, 150, 152
Men's studies, 143–52
*Men's Studies Newsletter,* 145
Miller, John W., 143–44, 146, 150
Mishnah, 72
*Momism: The Silent Disease of America* (Sebold), 119, 131
Monogamy, 30; *see also* Marital fidelity
Mother-child bond, 17, 47
Mothers, 4, 17, 102, 103, 128; as teachers, 69; transformation into, 14
*Mothers Are People Too* (Spencer), 132

Nash, John, 96
Neumann, Erich, 90
New Testament, 78–82; gospels, 73–78
Nietzsche, Friedrich, 110–11

*Odyssey* (Homer), 148
Oedipus complex, 96, 97, 98, 99, 105, 107, 108
*Origin of the Family, Private Property and the State, The* (Engels), 147
Original sin, 124
Osherson, Samuel, 132

Osiris, 40–41
Ostrovsky, Everett S., 148

Parke, Ross D., 149
Parke-Taylor, G. H., 42
Passover, 62–64, 70, 82
Patai, Raphael, 52
*Patria potestas,* 27, 80
Patriarchy, 3, 4, 5, 45–47, 146–47, 151; reproductive theory and, 19–22
Paul, 73, 78–79, 81
Peters, Ted, 114–15
Philo, 21
Plato, 113, 114
Plutarch, 28, 65–66
Polygamy, 26
Priest, John, 41
Prostitution, 26
Psychoanalysis, 104–09
Punishment, corporal, 102

Redemption of first born, 58–60, 70, 82
*Refusing to be a Man* (Stoltenberg), 148
Remarriage, 25
Reproduction, 4–5, 13, 19–22
*Republic, The* (Plato), 113
Research psychology, 87–88, 95–100
Rich, Adrienne, 146, 148
Rituals, 56, 57–64, 70, 82, 129, 131–32
*Role of the Father in Child Development, The,* 146, 149

Roman, Mel, 145
Ruether, Rosemary, 111, 112

Sacrifice, child. *See* Child
  sacrifice
Same-sex marriage, 151
Schüssler Fiorenza, Elisabeth,
  111–12
Sebold, Hans, 119, 131, 132
Secunda, Victoria, 148
Semen, 4, 18, 20
*Sexism and God-Talk, Toward
  a Feminist Theology*
  (Reuther), 111
Sexual bond, 13, 16–17,
  26–27, 117, 122; *see also*
  Marital bond
Sexual identity. *See* Gender
  identity
Socarides, 97–98
*Social Teaching of the
  Christian Churches, The*
  (Troeltsch), 123–24
Speiser, E. A., 137
Spencer, Anita, 132
Spouse abuse, 31; *see also*
  Wife abuse
Stein, Edward, 100
Stoltenberg, John, 148
Stoneberg, Theodore, 130–31

Talmud, 72
Tennis, Diane, 130
Tessman, Lora, 99
*Train Up a Child:
  Educational Ideals in the
  Ancient World* (Barclay), 65
Trible, Phyllis, 45–46, 48,
  49–50, 51, 52
Troeltsch, Ernst, 123–24

Vergote, Antoine, 47, 100
Virginity, 26; *see also*
  Celibacy

Weber, Hans-Ruedi, 74
Wellisch, Erich, 138–41
*Where the Two Came to
  Their Father,* 148
Wife abuse, 23, 24–26, 31
Wilson, Peter, 14, 117–18
*Women and Their Fathers:
  The Sexual and Romantic
  Impact of the First Man in
  Your Life* (Secunda), 148

Yahweh, 42, 43, 59, 60, 68,
  123; identification with El,
  52, 115–16; as male, 47,
  52; as midwife or mother,
  50–51

Zihlman, Andrienne, 89